knitted noah's ark

A collection of charming characters to recreate the story

Dedicated to Ruth,
Rebecca, Rachel,
Esther and Anna

First published 2012 by
Guild of Master Craftsman Publications Ltd
Castle Place, 166 High Street, Lewes,
East Sussex BN7 1XU

Reprinted 2013

ISBN 978 1 86108 915 1

A catalogue record for this book is available from
the British Library.

Publisher Jonathan Bailey
Production Manager Jim Bulley
Managing Editor Gerrie Purcell
Senior Project Editor Dominique Page
Editor Nicola Hodgson
Managing Art Editor Gilda Pacitti
Designer and photographer Rebecca Mothersole
Illustrator Simon Rodway

Set in Frutiger
Colour origination by GMC Reprographics
Printed and bound in China

The story of Noah's ark

Long ago, Noah, who was a kind and caring man, was told by God that He was unhappy with how wicked the rest of the world had become, so He had decided He would destroy all living creatures and start again. Noah was the only good man, so God decided to save him and his family. He told Noah that a great flood would come and cover the land and that Noah should build a wooden ark big enough for him, his family and two of every kind of animal and bird. Noah worked tirelessly to complete the ark, even though his friends mocked him, and by the time he was finished it was huge!

Then the rain came. What a storm! The rain poured down for 40 days and 40 nights without stopping. Floodwaters poured over towns and villages. Even the mountains were under water. The ark rolled back and forth on the stormy seas but Noah, his family and the animals were safe inside.

At last the rain stopped, and slowly the waters went down. The ark came to rest on a mountain, on top of Mount Ararat. Noah sent out a raven. It did not return as it had found a place to settle. A week later Noah sent out a dove. The dove returned with an olive leaf in its beak. Noah knew the dove had found dry land.

Finally God said to Noah, "Come out of the ark, you and your wife and your family. Bring out all the animals and birds so they can multiply on the earth and increase in number." The sun shone in the sky. All of the animals came out of the ark to begin their new lives in the new world. At the same time a rainbow appeared in the sky. God said, "This is a sign of my promise to you. I will never flood the whole world again."

knitted noah's ark

Where you'll find the characters

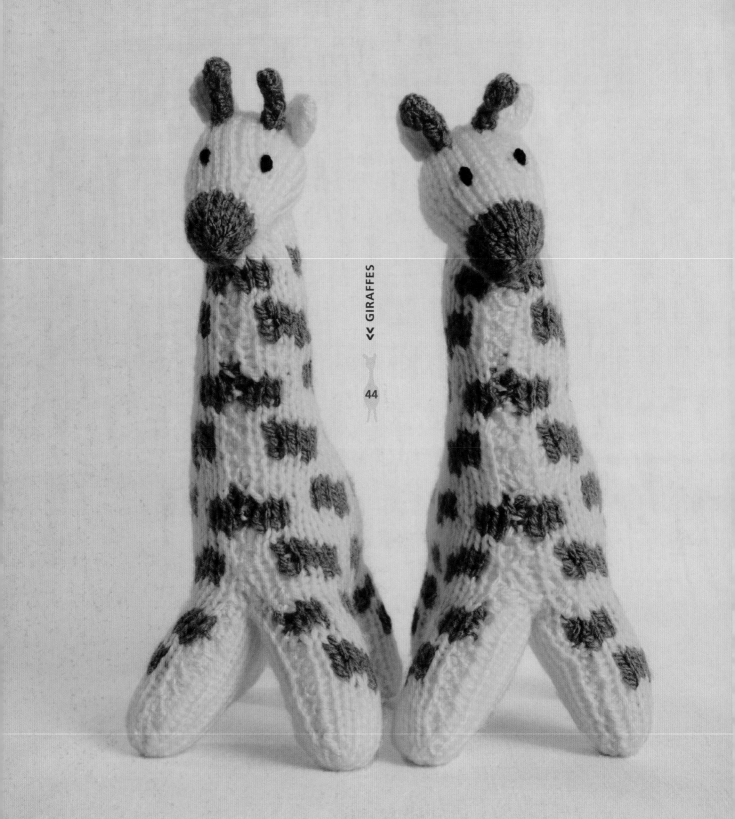

PENGUINS >>

74

94   << OWLS

**Some other animals
on Noah's checklist:**

Mr and Mrs Fox, friends and associates of Mr and Mrs Wolf,

Mr and Mrs Salmon, Mr and Mrs Cockatoo,

Mr and Mrs Swan, **Mr and Mrs Brown Bear.**

The projects

LIONS

Information you'll need

Finished size

Lions measure 4in (10cm) high

Materials

Any DK (US: light worsted) yarn
(NB: amounts are approximate)
50g gold (A)
10g mustard (B)
Oddment of black (C) for features
1 pair of 3.25mm (UK10:US3) needles
and 1 spare needle the same size
Knitters' blunt-ended pins and a needle
for sewing up
Acrylic toy stuffing

Tension

26 sts x 34 rows to 4in (10cm) square over
st st using 3.25mm needles and DK yarn
before stuffing.

Special abbreviation

Loop st: Insert RH needle into next st, place
first finger of LH behind LH needle and wind
yarn clockwise around needle and finger
twice, then just around needle once. Knit
this st, pulling 3 loops through. Place loops
just made onto LH needle and knit into the
back of them. Pull loops just made sharply
down to secure. Cont to next st.

How to make Lion

Legs and Body (make 2 pieces)

First leg

*Using the thumb method and A, cast on 6 sts.

Row 1 (WS): Purl.

Row 2: K1, m1, k4, m1, k1 (8 sts).
Beg with a p row, work 7 rows in st st.
Break yarn and set aside.

Second leg

Work as for first leg but do not break yarn.

Join legs

With RS facing, k across sts of second leg, turn and using the cable method cast on 10 sts, turn and with the same yarn cont knitting across sts of first leg (26 sts).
Beg with a p row, work 3 rows in st st. **
Place a marker on first and last st of last row.
Work 10 rows in st st.

Next row: K2tog, k to last 2 sts, k2tog tbl (24 sts).

Next row: P2tog tbl, p to last 2 sts, p2tog (22 sts).
Rep last 2 rows twice (14 sts).
Cast off.

Legs and Gusset (make 2 pieces)

Work as Legs and Body from * to **.
Cast off.

Head and Mane

Beg at centre front using the thumb method and A, cast on 8 sts.

Row 1 and foll 2 alt rows (WS): Purl.

Row 2: (Inc 1) to end (16 sts).

Row 4: (Inc 1, k1) to end (24 sts).

Row 6: (Inc 1, k2) to end (32 sts).
Beg with a p row, work 3 rows in st st.
Change to B for mane and k 1 row.

Loop-st row: K1, (loop-st) to last st, k1.
Rep last 2 rows once.

Row 14: (K2tog, k2) to end (24 sts).

Rep loop-st row once.

Row 16: (K2tog, k1) to end (16 sts).

Row 17: Purl.

Row 18: (K2tog) to end (8 sts).
Thread yarn through sts on needle, pull tight and secure by threading yarn a second time through sts.

Nose

Using the thumb method and C, cast on 5 sts.

Row 1 (WS): P1, p3tog, p1 (3 sts).

Row 2: Knit.
Thread yarn through sts on needle, pull tight and secure by threading yarn a second time through sts.

Ears (make 2)

Using the thumb method and A, cast on 7 sts.
Beg with a p row, work 3 rows in st st.

Row 4 (RS): K1, k2tog, k1, k2tog, k1 (5 sts).
Thread yarn through sts on needle, pull tight and secure by threading yarn a second time through sts.

Tail

Using the thumb method and A, cast on 12 sts for WS facing for first row.
Beg with a p row, work 4 rows in st st, ending on a k row.
Cast off p-wise.

Making up

Body

Place right sides of body together, matching all edges. Sew around top edge from marker to marker. Do not remove markers yet. Turn right side out.

Legs and Gusset

With right sides together, place one set of legs and gusset on outside of one side of lion, matching all edges. Sew around legs from marker to marker. Repeat for the other side. Turn legs right side out. Stuff each leg, then stuff the body and sew up the tummy seam.

Head and Mane

Gather round cast-on stitches of head, pull tight and secure. Join row ends of head leaving a gap, stuff, and close the gap. Pin and sew head to lion.

Nose

Sew nose to centre front of head.

Ears

Join row ends of ears and with this seam at centre back, sew ears to head.

Tail

Make a tassel in B approx. 2in (5cm) long with approx. 20 strands in tassel (see p. 122). Sew the head of the tassel securely to the wrong side of the inside edge of one end of the tail. Join cast-on and cast-off stitches of tail around the head of the tassel and along the tail. Trim tassel to ½in (1.5cm). Sew tail to lion at back.

Features

To make eyes, take two lengths of black yarn and tie a knot in each, winding yarn round five times to make the knots (see p. 122). Mark position of eyes on lion. Tie eyes to head and run ends into head. Embroider mouth using straight stitches, as shown in picture on the right (see p. 122 for beginning and fastening off embroidery invisibly).

How to make Lioness

Make Legs, Body, Gusset, Nose, Ears and Tail in A as for lion. Work head for lioness as foll:

Head

Beg at centre front of head using the thumb method and A, cast on 9 sts.
Row 1 and foll 2 alt rows (WS): Purl.
Row 2: (Inc 1) to end (18 sts).
Row 4: (Inc 1, k1) to end (27 sts).
Row 6: (Inc 1, k2) to end (36 sts).
Beg with a p row, work 9 rows in st st.
Shape head
Row 16: (K2tog, k2) to end (27 sts).
Row 17 and foll alt row: Purl.
Row 18: (K2tog, k1) to end (18 sts).
Row 20: (K2tog) to end (9 sts).
Thread yarn through sts on needle, pull tight and secure by threading yarn a second time through sts.

Making up

Make up as for lion, omitting mane, and work tassel for tail in A.

TIGERS

Information you'll need

Finished size
Tigers measure 4in (10cm) high

Materials
Any DK (US: light worsted) yarn
(NB: amounts are approximate)
30g burnt orange (A)
30g black (B)
5g white (C)
Oddment of grey for features
1 pair of 3.25mm (UK10:US3) needles
and 1 spare needle the same size
Knitters' blunt-ended pins and a needle
for sewing up
Acrylic toy stuffing
2 pipe cleaners

Tension
26 sts x 34 rows to 4in (10cm) square over
st st using 3.25mm needles and DK yarn
before stuffing.

Row 32: Using A, k15, (k2tog) twice, k2, (k2tog) twice, k15 (36 sts).
Row 33: Using A, purl.
Row 34: Using B, k13, (k2tog) twice, k2, (k2tog) twice, k13 (32 sts).
Row 35: Using B, purl.
Row 36: Using A, knit.
Place markers on 10th and 23rd st of last row and keep markers on RS.
Using A, cast off p-wise.

Legs and Gusset (make 2 pieces)
First leg
Using the thumb method and A, cast on 7 sts for WS facing for first row.
Beg with a p row, work 7 rows in st st. Break yarn and set aside.
Second leg
Work as for first leg but do not break yarn.
Join legs
With RS facing, k across sts of second leg, turn and using the cable method cast on 10 sts, turn and with the same yarn cont knitting across sts of first leg (24 sts).
Beg with a p row, work 3 rows in st st. Cast off.

Head
Beg at centre back using the thumb method and B, cast on 9 sts.
Row 1 (WS): Purl.
Row 2: (Inc 1) to end (18 sts).
Join on A and work in st st in stripe carrying yarn loosely up side of work.
Row 3: Using A, purl.
Row 4: Using A, (inc 1, k1) to end (27 sts).
Row 5: Using B, purl.
Row 6: Using B, (inc 1, k2) to end (36 sts).
Join on C and work in intarsia, twisting yarn when changing colours to avoid a hole.
Row 7: Using A, p20, using C, p16.
Row 8: Using C, k16, using A, k20.
Row 9: Using B, p20, using C, p16.

Row 10: Using C, k16, using B, k20.
Rep rows 7–10 once, then row 7 once.
Shape head
Row 16: Using C, (k2tog, k2) 4 times, using A, (k2tog, k2) 5 times (27 sts).
Row 17: Using B, p15, using C, p12.
Row 18: Using C, (k2tog, k1) 4 times, using B, (k2tog, k1) 5 times (18 sts).
Row 19: Using A, p10, using C, p8.
Row 20: Using C, (k2tog) 4 times, using A, (k2tog) 5 times (9 sts).
Thread yarn through sts on needle, pull tight and secure by threading yarn a second time through sts.

Nose
Using the thumb method and B, cast on 6 sts.
Row 1 (WS): P2tog tbl, p2, p2tog (4 sts).
Thread yarn through sts on needle, pull tight and secure by threading yarn a second time through sts.

Ears (make 2)
Using the thumb method and B, cast on 8 sts.
Row 1 (WS): Purl.
Row 2: (K2tog) 4 times (4 sts).
Thread yarn through sts on needle, pull tight and secure by threading yarn a second time through sts.

Tail
Using the thumb method and B, cast on 6 sts for WS facing for first row.
Purl 1 row.
Join on A and work in st st in stripe carrying yarn loosely up side of work; work 18 rows in stripe starting with 2 rows in A, then 2 rows in B and do this alternately, finishing with 2 rows in A.
Thread yarn through sts on needle, pull tight and secure by threading yarn a second time through sts.

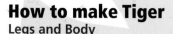

How to make Tiger
Legs and Body
Beg at one end using the thumb method and A, cast on 32 sts.
Place markers on 10th and 23rd sts of sts just cast on and keep markers on RS.
Row 1 (WS): Purl.
Join on B and work in st st in stripe carrying yarn loosely up side of work; shape as foll:
Row 2: Using B, k14, (m1, k1) twice, (k1, m1) twice, k14 (36 sts).
Row 3: Using B, purl.
Row 4: Using A, k16, (m1, k1) twice, (k1, m1) twice, k16 (40 sts).
Row 5: Using A, purl.
Using B, work 2 rows in st st.
Row 8: Using A, knit.
Row 9: Using A, cast off 7 sts p-wise, p25 (26 sts now on RH needle), cast off rem 7 sts p-wise and fasten off (26 sts).
Rejoin A and B and work 18 rows in st st in stripe, 2 rows in B, then 2 rows in A; do this alternately, finishing with 2 rows in B.
Using A and the cable method, cast on 7 sts at beg of next 2 rows (40 sts).
Rejoin B and using B, work 2 rows in st st.

Making up

Body

With right side of stocking-stitch outside, fold body in half bringing legs together; join cast-on stitches and cast-off stitches from fold to markers. Do not remove markers yet.

Legs and Gusset

With right sides together, place one set of legs and gusset on outside of one side of tiger, matching all edges. Sew around legs from marker to marker. Repeat for other side. Turn legs right side out. Stuff each leg, then stuff the body and sew up the tummy seam.

Head

Join row ends of head from nose to end of white part, sewing back and forth one stitch in from edge on wrong side. Stuff head and gather round cast-on stitches of head, pull tight and secure and join remainder of row ends. Pin and sew head to tiger.

Nose

Sew nose to centre front of head.

Ears

Join row ends of ears; with this seam at centre back, sew ears to head.

Tail

Take a pipe cleaner and fold in half. Cut pipe cleaner to length of tail and place folded end into wrong side of stitches pulled tight on a thread. Using mattress stitch (see p. 121), join row ends of tail around pipe cleaner. Sew tail to tiger at back and curl tip of tail outwards.

Features

To make eyes, take two lengths of grey yarn and tie a knot in each, winding yarn round five times to make the knots (see p. 122). Mark position of eyes on tiger. Tie eyes to head and run ends into head. Embroider mouth in B using straight stitches, as shown in picture on p. 32 (see p. 122 for starting and finishing off embroidery invisibly).

ELEPHANTS

Information you'll need

Finished size
Elephants measure 4¾in (12cm) high

Materials
Any DK (US: light worsted) yarn
(NB: amounts are approximate)
60g grey (A)
5g white (B)
Oddment of black for features
1 pair of 3.25mm (UK10:US3) needles
and 2 spare needles the same size
Knitters' blunt-ended pins and a needle
for sewing up
Tweezers for stuffing small parts (optional)
Acrylic toy stuffing

Tension
26 sts x 34 rows to 4in (10cm) square over
st st using 3.25mm needles and DK yarn
before stuffing.

How to make Elephant

Left side of Legs, Body, Head and Trunk

Trunk

Using the thumb method and A, cast on 3 sts.

Beg with a p row, work 3 rows in st st.

Row 4 (RS): K2, m1, k1 (4 sts).

Row 5: Purl.

Row 6: K3, m1, k1 (5 sts).

Beg with a p row, work 7 rows in st st.

Row 14: K4, m1, k1 (6 sts).

Beg with a p row, work 7 rows in st st.

Row 22: K1, m1, k to end (7 sts).

Row 23: Purl.

Rep last 2 rows once (8 sts).

Break yarn and set aside.

First leg

*Using the thumb method and A, cast on 6 sts.

Row 1 (WS): Purl.

Row 2: K1, m1, k4, m1, k1 (8 sts).

Beg with a p row, work 9 rows in st st.

Break yarn and set aside.

Second leg

Work as for first leg but do not break yarn.

Join legs

With RS facing, k across sts of second leg, turn and using the cable method cast on 10 sts, turn and with the same yarn cont knitting across sts of first leg (26 sts).

Beg with a p row, work 3 rows in st st. Place a marker on first and last sts of last row.

Work 8 rows in st st. **

Next row: K to last st, m1, k1 (27 sts).

Next row: Purl.

Rep last 2 rows once (28 sts).

Join trunk and body

With RS facing, k across sts of body and then with the same yarn cont knitting across sts of trunk (36 sts).

Beg with a p row, work 5 rows in st st.

Next row: K2tog, k to end (35 sts).

Next row: Purl.

Rep last 2 rows once (34 sts).

Next row: Cast off 4 sts at beg of next row and k to last 2 sts, k2tog tbl (29 sts).

Next row: P2tog tbl, p to end (28 sts).

Rep last 2 rows 4 times more (4 sts).

Cast off rem 4 sts.

Right side of Legs, Body, Head and Trunk

Work as Left side of Legs, Body, Head and Trunk from * to **.

Next row: K1, m1, k to end (27 sts).

Next row: Purl.

Rep last 2 rows once (28 sts).

Break yarn and set aside.

Trunk

Using the thumb method and A, cast on 3 sts.

Beg with a p row, work 3 rows in st st.

Row 4 (RS): K1, m1, k2 (4 sts).

Row 5: Purl.

Row 6: K1, m1, k3 (5 sts).

Beg with a p row, work 7 rows in st st.

Row 14: K1, m1, k4 (6 sts).

Beg with a p row, work 7 rows in st st.

Row 22: K to last st, m1, k1 (7 sts).

Row 23: Purl.

Rep last 2 rows once (8 sts).

Join trunk and body

With RS facing, k across sts of trunk, then with the same yarn cont knitting across sts of body (36 sts).

Beg with a p row, work 5 rows in st st.

Next row: K to last 2 sts, k2tog tbl (35 sts).

Next row: Purl.

Rep last 2 rows once (34 sts).

Knit 1 row.

Next row: Cast off 4 sts p-wise, p to last 2 sts, p2tog (29 sts).

Next row: K2tog, k to end (28 sts).

Rep last 2 rows 4 times more (4 sts).

Cast of rem 4 sts p-wise.

Legs and Gusset (make 2 pieces)

First leg

Using the thumb method and A, cast on 6 sts.

Row 1 (WS): Purl.

Row 2: K1, m1, k4, m1, k1 (8 sts).

Beg with a p row, work 9 rows in st st.

Break yarn and set aside.

Second leg

Work as for first leg but do not break yarn.

Join legs

With RS facing, k across sts of second leg, turn and using the cable method cast on 10 sts, turn and with the same yarn cont knitting across sts of first leg (26 sts).
Beg with a p row, work 3 rows in st st.
Cast off.

Ears (make 4 pieces)

Using the thumb method and A, cast on 8 sts.
Row 1 (WS): Purl.
Row 2: (K1, m1) twice, k to last 2 sts, (m1, k1) twice (12 sts).
Rep first 2 rows once (16 sts).
Beg with a p row, work 3 rows in st st.
Row 8: (K2tog) twice, k to last 4 sts, k2tog, k2tog tbl (12 sts).
Row 9: Purl.
Rep last 2 rows once (8 sts).
Row 12: (K2tog) 3 times, k2tog tbl (4 sts).
Cast off p-wise.

Tail

Using the thumb method and A, cast on 12 sts for WS facing for first row.
Beg with a p row, work 4 rows in st st, ending on a k row.
Cast off p-wise.

Tusks (make 2)

Using the thumb method and B, cast on 9 sts.
Beg with a p row, work 3 rows in st st.
Row 4 (RS): K2tog, k to last 2 sts, k2tog tbl (7 sts).
Row 5: Purl.
Rep last 2 rows twice more (3 sts).
Thread yarn through sts on needle, pull tight and secure by threading yarn a second time through sts.

Making up

Body, Head and Trunk

Place right sides of body pieces together, matching all edges. Sew from tip of trunk, up outside edge of trunk, over head, across back, and down as far as the markers at the back. Do not remove markers yet. Turn right side out. Sew up inside edge of trunk by oversewing on right side, pushing a little stuffing into the trunk with tweezers or tip of scissors as you sew. Sew round chin to markers at front. Curl tip of trunk by sewing a gathering stitch along inside edge of trunk, pull tight and secure.

Legs and Gusset

With right sides together, place one set of legs and gusset on outside of one side of elephant, matching all edges. Sew around legs from marker to marker. Repeat for the other side. Turn legs right side out. Stuff each leg, then stuff the head and back and sew up the tummy seam.

Ears

Place right sides of two pieces of ear together, matching all edges. Sew around row ends and cast-off stitches by sewing back and forth one stitch in from edge. Repeat for other ear and turn both ears right side out. Join cast-on stitches of each ear. Pin and sew cast-on stitches of ears to head.

Tusks

Roll each tusk up from row ends to row ends and sew in place. Curl tusks by sewing a gathering stitch from base edge to tip, pull tight and secure by sewing back to base edge and secure. Sew base edge of tusks to elephant.

Tail

Make a tassel in A approx. 2in (5cm) long with approx. 18 strands in tassel (see p. 122). Sew head of tassel securely to wrong side of inside edge of one end of tail. Join cast-on and cast-off stitches of tail around head of tassel and along the tail. Trim tassel to ½in (1.5cm). Sew tail to elephant at back.

Features

To make eyes, take two lengths of black yarn and tie a knot in each, winding yarn round four times to make the knots (see p. 122). Mark position of eyes on elephant. Tie eyes to head, one to each side and run ends into head.

HIPPOS

Information you'll need

Finished size
Hippos measure 4in (10cm) high

Materials
Any DK (US: light worsted) yarn
(NB: amounts are approximate)
60g grey-blue (A)
Oddment of black for features
1 pair of 3.25mm (UK10:US3) needles
and 1 spare needle the same size
Knitters' blunt-ended pins and a needle
for sewing up
Acrylic toy stuffing

Tension
26 sts x 34 rows to 4in (10cm) square
over st st using 3.25mm needles and
DK yarn before stuffing.

How to make Hippo

Legs and Body (make 2 pieces)

First leg
*Using the thumb method and A, cast on 6 sts.

Row 1 (WS): Purl.

Row 2: K1, m1, k4, m1, k1 (8 sts).

Beg with a p row, work 5 rows in st st. Break yarn and set aside.

Second leg
Work as for first leg but do not break yarn.

Join legs
With RS facing, k across sts of second leg, turn and using the cable method cast on 12 sts, turn and with the same yarn cont knitting across sts of first leg (28 sts).

Beg with a p row, work 3 rows in st st. **

Place marker on first and last sts of last row. Work 12 rows in st st.

Next row: K2tog, k to last 2 sts, k2tog tbl (26 sts).

Next row: P2tog tbl, p to last 2 sts, p2tog (24 sts).

Rep last 2 rows twice (16 sts).

Cast off.

Legs and Gusset (make 2 pieces)
Work as Legs and Body from * to **.

Cast off.

Head
Using the thumb method and A, cast on 14 sts. Place a marker at centre of cast-on sts.

Row 1 (WS): Purl.

Row 2: K2, (m1, k1) 5 times, (k1, m1) 5 times, k2 (24 sts).

Beg with a p row, work 13 rows in st st.

Shape top of head

Row 16: (K2tog, k1) to end (16 sts).

Row 17: Purl.

Row 18: (K2tog) to end (8 sts).

Thread yarn through sts on needle, pull tight and secure by threading yarn a second time through sts.

Muzzle
Using the thumb method and A, cast on 22 sts.

Beg with a p row, work 3 rows in st st.

Row 4 (RS): (K5, m1, k1, m1, k5) twice (26 sts).

Row 5: Purl.

Row 6: (K6, m1, k1, m1, k6) twice (30 sts).

Beg with a p row, work 7 rows in st st.

Row 14: *K2, (k2tog, k1) 4 times, k1, rep from * once (22 sts).

Row 15: Purl.

Row 16: *K1, (k2tog) twice, k1, (k2tog) twice, k1, rep from * once (14 sts).

Cast off p-wise.

Ears (make 2)
Using the thumb method and A, cast on 7 sts.

Beg with a p row, work 3 rows in st st.

Row 4 (RS): K1, (k2tog, k1) twice (5 sts).

Thread yarn through sts on needle, pull tight and secure by threading yarn a second time through sts.

Tail
Using the thumb method and A, cast on 6 sts.

Beg with a p row, work 5 rows in st st.

Row 6 (RS): K2, k2tog, k2 (5 sts).

Beg with a p row, work 3 rows in st st. Thread yarn through sts on needle, pull tight and secure by threading yarn a second time through sts.

Making up

Body
Place right sides of body together, matching all edges. Sew around top edge from marker to marker. Do not remove markers yet. Turn right side out.

Legs and Gusset
With right sides together, place one set of legs and gusset on outside of one side of hippo, matching all edges. Sew around legs from marker to marker. Repeat for the other side. Turn legs right side out. Stuff each leg, then stuff the body and sew up the tummy seam.

Head and Muzzle
Join row ends of head and stuff the head. Bring seam and marker together and oversew cast-on stitches. Join row ends of muzzle and with this seam at centre of underneath edge, join the cast-off stitches. Stuff the muzzle and sew the cast-on stitches of the muzzle to the head all the way round, sewing the lower edge of the muzzle to the lower edge of the head. Pin and sew head to body.

Ears
Join row ends of ears; with this seam at centre back, sew ears to head.

Tail
Join row ends of tail. Sew tail to hippo at back.

Features
To make eyes, take two lengths of black yarn and tie a knot in each, winding yarn round four times to make the knots (see p. 122). Mark position of eyes on hippo. Tie eyes to head and run ends into head. Work two nostrils on muzzle using black yarn, making two short stitches close together for each nostril, as shown in picture on right (see p. 122 for beginning and fastening off embroidery invisibly).

GIRAFFES

Information you'll need

Finished size
Giraffes measure 8in (20cm) high

Materials
Any DK (US: light worsted) yarn
(NB: amounts are approximate)
60g yellow (A)
30g brown (B)
5g dark brown (C)
Oddment of black for features
1 pair of 3.25mm (UK10:US3) needles
and 1 spare needle the same size
Knitters' blunt-ended pins and a needle
for sewing up
Acrylic toy stuffing

Tension
26 sts x 34 rows to 4in (10cm) square over
st st using 3.25mm needles and DK yarn
before stuffing.

How to make Giraffe

Left side of Legs, Body and Neck

First leg

Using the thumb method and A, cast on 6 sts.

Row 1 (WS): Purl.

Row 2: K1, m1, k to last st, m1, k1 (8 sts). Beg with a p row, work 5 rows in st st. Join on B and work with A and B in Fair Isle, carrying yarn loosely across back of work and twisting yarn when changing colours to avoid a hole.

Row 8: Using A, k2, using B, k2, using A, k4.

Row 9: Using A, p2, using B, p4, using A, p2.

Row 10: Using A, k2, using B, k4, using A, k2.

Row 11: Using A, p2, using B, p2, using A, p4.

Row 12: Using A, knit.

Row 13: Using A, purl.

Row 14: Using B, k1, using A, k4, using B, k2, using A, k1.

Row 15: Using B, p3, using A, p2, using B, p3.

Row 16: Using B, k3, using A, k2, using B, k3.

Row 17: Using B, p1, using A, p4, using B, p2, using A, p1.
Break yarn and set aside.

Second leg

Work as for first leg but do not break yarn.

Join legs

With RS facing and using A, k across sts of second leg, turn and using the cable method cast on 10 sts, turn and with the same yarn cont knitting across sts of first leg (26 sts).

Using A, purl 1 row.

Work body

Row 1: Using A, k2, (using B, k2, using A, k4) 4 times.

Row 2: Using A, p2, (using B, p4, using A, p2) 4 times.
Place a marker on first and last sts of last row.

Row 3: Using A, k2, (using B, k4, using A, k2) 4 times.

Row 4: Using A, p2, (using B, p2, using A, p4) 4 times.

Row 5: Using A, knit.

Row 6: Using A, purl.

Row 7: Using B, k1, (using A, k4, using B, k2) 4 times, using A, k1.

Row 8: Using B, p3, using A, p2, (using B, p4, using A, p2) 3 times, using B, p3.

Row 9: Using B, k3, using A, k2, (using B, k4, using A, k2) 3 times, using B, k3.

Row 10: Using B, p1, (using A, p4, using B, p2) 4 times, using A, p1.

Shape back

Row 11: Using A, (k2tog) twice, k to end (24 sts).

Row 12: Using A, p to last 2 sts, p2tog (23 sts).

Row 13: Using A, (k2tog) twice, k1, (using B, k2, using A, k4) 3 times (21 sts).

Row 14: (Using A, p2, using B, p4) 3 times, using A, p1, p2tog (20 sts).

Row 15: Using A, k2tog, using B, k2tog, k2, using A, k2, (using B, k4, using A, k2) twice (18 sts).

Row 16: Using A, p2, using B, p2, (using A, p4, using B, p2) twice, using A, p2tog (17 sts).

Row 17: Using A, (k2tog) twice, k to end (15 sts).

Row 18: Using A, p to last 2 sts, p2tog (14 sts).

Row 19: Using A, (k2tog) twice, k1, using B, k2, using A, k4, using B, k2, using A, k1 (12 sts).

Row 20: Using B, p3, using A, p2, using B, p4, using A, p1, p2tog (11 sts).

Row 21: Using A, k2, using B, k4, using A, k2, using B, k3.

Row 22: Using B, p1, using A, p4, using B, p2, using A, p4.

Row 23: Using A, knit.

Row 24: Using A, purl.

Row 25: Using B, k1, using A, k4, using B, k2, using A, k4.

Row 26: Using A, p2, using B, p4, using A, p2, using B, p3.

Row 27: Using B, k3, using A, k2, using B, k4, using A, k2.

Row 28: Using A, p2, using B, p2, using A, p4, using B, p2, using A, p1.

Row 29: Using A, knit.

Row 30: Using A, purl.

Row 31: Using A, k2tog, using B, k2, using A, k4, using B, k2, using A, k1 (10 sts).

Row 32: Using B, p3, using A, p2, using B, p4, using A, p1.

Row 33: Using A, k1, using B, k4, using A, k2, using B, k3.

Row 34: Using B, p1, using A, p4, using B, p2, using A, p3.

Row 35: Using A, knit.

Row 36: Using A, cast off 3 sts p-wise, p to end (7 sts).

Row 37: Using A, knit.

Row 38: As row 36 (4 sts).
Cast off rem 4 sts.

Right side of Legs, Body and Neck

First leg

Using the thumb method and A, cast on 6 sts.

Row 1 (WS): Purl.

Row 2: K1, m1, k to last st, m1, k1 (8 sts). Beg with a p row, work 5 rows in st st. Join on B and work with A and B in Fair Isle, carrying yarn loosely across back of work and twisting yarn when changing colours to avoid a hole.

Row 8: Using A, k4, using B, k2, using A, k2.

Row 9: Using A, p2, using B, p4, using A, p2.

Row 10: Using A, k2, using B, k4, using A, k2.

Row 11: Using A, p4, using B, p2, using A, p2.

Row 12: Using A, knit.

Row 13: Using A, purl.

Row 14: Using A, k1, using B, k2, using A, k4, using B, k1.

Row 15: Using B, p3, using A, p2, using B, p3.

Row 16: Using B, k3, using A, k2, using B, k3.

Row 17: Using A, p1, using B, p2, using A, p4, using B, p1.

Break yarn and set aside.

Second leg

Work as for first leg but do not break yarn.

Join legs

With RS facing and using A, k across sts of second leg, turn and using the cable method cast on 10 sts, turn and with the same yarn cont knitting across sts of first leg (26 sts).

Using A, purl 1 row.

Work body

Row 1: (Using A, k4, using B, k2) 4 times, using A, k2.

Row 2: (Using A, p2, using B, p4) 4 times, using A, p2.

Place a marker on first and last sts of last row.

Row 3: (Using A, k2, using B, k4) 4 times, using A, k2.

Row 4: (Using A, p4, using B, p2) 4 times, using A, p2.

Row 5: Using A, knit.

Row 6: Using A, purl.

Row 7: Using A, k1, (using B, k2, using A, k4) 4 times, using B, k1.

Row 8: Using B, p3, (using A, p2, using B, p4) 3 times, using A, p2, using B, p3.

Row 9: Using B, k3, (using A, k2, using B,

k4) 3 times, using A, k2, using B, k3.

Row 10: Using A, p1, (using B, p2, using A, p4) 4 times, using B, p1.

Shape back

Row 11: Using A, k to last 4 sts, k2tog, k2tog tbl (24 sts).

Row 12: Using A, p2tog tbl, p to end (23 sts).

Row 13: (Using A, k4, using B, k2) 3 times, using A, k1, k2tog, k2tog tbl (21 sts).

Row 14: Using A, p2tog tbl, p1, (using B, p4, using A, p2) 3 times (20 sts).

Row 15: (Using A, k2, using B, k4) twice, using A, k2, using B, k2, k2tog, using A, k2tog tbl (18 sts).

Row 16: Using A, p2tog tbl, (using B, p2, using A, p4) twice, using B, p2, using A, p2 (17 sts).

Row 17: Using A, k to last 4 sts, k2tog, k2tog tbl (15 sts).

Row 18: Using A, p2tog tbl, p to end (14 sts).

Row 19: Using A, k1, using B, k2, using A, k4, using B, k2, using A, k1, k2tog, k2tog tbl (12 sts).

Row 20: Using A, p2tog tbl, p1, using B, p4, using A, p2, using B, p3 (11 sts).

Row 21: Using B, k3, using A, k2, using B, k4, using A, k2.

Row 22: Using A, p4, using B, p2, using A, p4, using B, p1.

Row 23: Using A, knit.

Row 24: Using A, purl.

Row 25: Using A, k4, using B, k2, using A, k4, using B, k1.

Row 26: Using B, p3, using A, p2, using B, p4, using A, p2.

Row 27: Using A, k2, using B, k4, using A, k2, using B, k3.

Row 28: Using A, p1, using B, p2, using A, p4, using B, p2, using A, p2.

Row 29: Using A, knit.

Row 30: Using A, purl.

Row 31: Using A, k1, using B, k2, using A, k4, using B, k2, using A, k2tog tbl (10 sts).

Row 32: Using A, p1, using B, p4, using A, p2, using B, p3.

Row 33: Using B, k3, using A, k2, using B, k4, using A, k1.

Row 34: Using A, p3, using B, p2, using A, p4, using B, p1.

Row 35: Using A, cast off 3 sts at beg of row and k to end (7 sts).

Row 36: Using A, purl.

Row 37: As row 35 (4 sts).

Row 38: Using A, purl.

Cast off rem 4 sts.

Legs and Gusset (make 2 pieces)

First leg

Using the thumb method and A, cast on 6 sts.

Row 1 (WS): Purl.

Row 2: K1, m1, k4, m1, k1 (8 sts).

Beg with a p row, work 15 rows in st st.

Break yarn and set aside.

Second leg

Work as for first leg but do not break yarn.

Join legs

With RS facing, k across sts of second leg, turn and using the cable method, cast on 10 sts, turn and with the same yarn cont knitting across sts of first leg (26 sts).

Beg with a p row, work 3 rows in st st.

Cast off.

Head

Beg at back using the thumb method and A, cast on 8 sts.

Row 1 and foll alt row (WS): Purl.

Row 2: K1, (m1, k1) to end (15 sts).

Row 4: K1, (m1, k2) to end (22 sts).

Beg with a p row, work 7 rows in st st.

Row 12: (K3, k2tog, k1, k2tog, k3) twice (18 sts).

Row 13: Purl.

Row 14: (K2, k2tog, k1, k2tog, k2) twice (14 sts).

Beg with a p row, work 3 rows in st st.
Change to B.
Row 18: (K1 tbl) to end.
Beg with a p row, work 3 rows in st st.
Row 22: K2tog, (k1, k2tog) to end (9 sts).
Thread yarn through sts on needle,
pull tight and secure by threading yarn
a second time through sts.

Horns (make 2)
Using the thumb method and B, cast
on 3 sts.
Beg with a p row, work 3 rows in st st.
Row 4 (RS): K1, (m1, k1) twice (5 sts).
Row 5: Purl.
Thread yarn through sts on needle,
pull tight and secure by threading yarn
a second time through sts.

Ears (make 2)
Using the thumb method and A, cast
on 6 sts for WS facing for first row.
Beg with a p row, work 4 rows in st st,
ending on a K row.
Thread yarn through sts on needle,
pull tight and secure by threading yarn
a second time through sts.

Mane
Using the thumb method and C, cast on
20 sts for RS facing for first row and work
in garter st.
Work 5 rows in garter st.
Cast off loosely in garter st.

Tail
Using the thumb method and A, cast
on 10 sts for WS facing for first row.
Beg with a p row, work 4 rows in st st,
ending on a k row.
Cast off p-wise.

Making up
Body and Neck
Place right sides of body together,
matching all edges. Sew neck and back
seams from top edge as far down as
markers at front and back by sewing back
and forth one stitch in from edge. Do not
remove markers yet. Turn right side out.

Legs and Gusset
With right sides together, place one set of
legs and gusset on outside of one side
of giraffe, matching all edges. Sew around
legs from marker to marker. Repeat for the
other side. Turn legs right side out. Stuff
each leg, then stuff the neck and body and
sew up the tummy seam.

Head
Gather round cast-on stitches of head, pull
tight and secure. Join row ends of head,
leaving a gap. Stuff the head and close
the gap. Sew head to neck, adding more
stuffing to neck if needed.

Horns
Join row ends of horns and sew to top
of head.

Ears
Join row ends of ears and sew to head
at each side.

Mane
Join cast-on and cast-off stitches of
mane. Pin and sew to head and neck.

Tail
Make a tassel in A approx. 2in (5cm) long
with approx. 18 strands in tassel (see p. 122).
Sew head of tassel securely to wrong side of
inside edge of one end of tail. Join cast-on
and cast-off stitches of tail around head of
tassel and along the tail. Trim tassel to ½in
(1.5cm). Sew tail to giraffe at back.

Features
To make eyes, take two lengths of black
yarn and tie a knot in each, winding yarn
round four times to make the knots (see
p. 122). Mark position of eyes on giraffe.
Tie eyes to head and run ends into head.

ZEBRAS

Information you'll need

Finished size
Zebras measure 4½in (11.5cm) high

Materials
Any DK (US: light worsted) yarn
(NB: amounts are approximate)
30g white (A)
30g black (B)
1 pair of 3.25mm (UK10:US3) needles
and 1 spare needle the same size
Knitters' blunt-ended pins and a needle
for sewing up
Acrylic toy stuffing

Tension
26 sts x 34 rows to 4in (10cm) square over
st st using 3.25mm needles and DK yarn
before stuffing.

How to make Zebra

Legs and Body

Beg at one end using the thumb method and A, cast on 36 sts.

Place markers on 12th and 25th sts of sts just cast on and keep markers on RS.

Row 1 (WS): Purl.

Join on B and work in st st in stripe carrying yarn loosely up side of work; shape as foll:

Row 2: Using B, k16, (m1, k1) twice, (k1, m1) twice, k16 (40 sts).

Row 3: Using B, purl.

Row 4: Using A, k18, (m1, k1) twice, (k1, m1) twice, k18 (44 sts).

Row 5: Using A, purl.

Using B, work 2 rows in st st.

Row 8: Using A, knit.

Row 9: Using A, cast off 9 sts p-wise, p25 (26 sts now on RH needle), cast off rem 9 sts p-wise and fasten off (26 sts).

Rejoin A and B and work 14 rows in st st in stripe, 2 rows in B, then 2 rows in A; do this alternately, finishing with 2 rows in B. Using A and the cable method, cast on 9 sts at beg of next 2 rows (44 sts).

Rejoin B and using B, work 2 rows in st st.

Row 28: Using A, k17, (k2tog) twice, k2, (k2tog) twice, k17 (40 sts).

Row 29: Using A, purl.

Row 30: Using B, k15, (k2tog) twice, k2, (k2tog) twice, k15 (36 sts).

Row 31: Using B, purl.

Row 32: Using A, knit.

Place markers on 12th and 25th sts of last row and keep markers on RS.

Using A, cast off p-wise.

Legs and Gusset (make 2 pieces)

First leg

Using the thumb method and A, cast on 7 sts for WS facing for first row.

Beg with a p row, work 9 rows in st st.

Break yarn and set aside.

Second leg

Work as for first leg but do not break yarn.

Join legs

With RS facing, k across sts of second leg, turn and using the cable method cast on 12 sts, turn and with the same yarn cont knitting across sts of first leg (26 sts). Beg with a p row, work 3 rows in st st. Cast off.

Head

Beg at back using the thumb method and B, cast on 20 sts.

Row 1 (WS): Purl.

Join on A and work in st st in stripe carrying yarn loosely up side of work; shape as foll:

Row 2: Using A, k8, (m1, k1) twice, (k1, m1) twice, k8 (24 sts).

Row 3: Using A, purl.

Row 4: Using B, k10, (m1, k1) twice, (k1, m1) twice, k10 (28 sts).

Row 5: Using B, purl.

Work 6 rows in st st in stripe, 2 rows in A, 2 rows in B, then 2 rows in A.

Row 12: Using B, k10, (k2tog) 4 times, k10 (24 sts).

Row 13: Using B, cast off 4 sts p-wise, p15 (16 sts now on RH needle), cast off rem 4 sts and fasten off (16 sts).

Row 14: Rejoin A and B and using A, k 1 row.

Row 15: Using A, p2tog tbl, p to last 2 sts, p2tog (14 sts).

Using B, work 2 rows in st st.

Cont in A and work 4 rows in st st.

Row 22: (K2tog) to end (7 sts).

Thread yarn through sts on needle, pull tight and secure by threading yarn a second time through sts.

Mane

Using the thumb method and B, cast on 16 sts for RS facing for first row and work in garter st.

Work 5 rows in garter st.

Cast off in garter st.

Ears (make 2)

Using the thumb method and A, cast on 6 sts.

Beg with a p row, work 3 rows in st st.

Row 4 (RS): K1, (k2tog) twice, k1 (4 sts).

Thread yarn through sts on needle, pull tight and secure by threading yarn a second time through sts.

Tail

Using the thumb method and A, cast on 10 sts for WS facing for first row.

Beg with a p row, work 4 rows in st st, ending on a k row.

Cast off p-wise.

Making up

Body

With right side of stocking-stitch outside, fold body in half, bringing legs together; join cast-on stitches and cast-off stitches from fold to markers. Do not remove markers yet.

Legs and Gusset

With right sides together, place one set of legs and gusset on outside of one side of zebra, matching all edges. Sew around legs from marker to marker. Repeat for other side. Turn legs right side out. Stuff each leg, then stuff the body and sew up the tummy seam.

Head

Fold cast-on stitches of head in half and join. Join row ends of muzzle and cast-off stitches beneath chin. Stuff the head, pushing the stuffing into the muzzle and the top of the head. Pin and sew head to body, matching stripes.

Mane

Join cast-on and cast-off stitches of mane and sew the mane over head and down neck to back.

Ears

Join row ends of ears and sew cast-on stitches to each side of head.

Tail

Make a tassel in B approx. 2in (5cm) long with approx. 18 strands in tassel (see p. 122). Sew head of tassel securely to wrong side of inside edge of one end of tail. Join cast-on and cast-off stitches of tail around head of tassel and along the tail. Trim tassel to ½in (1.5cm). Sew tail to zebra at back.

Features

To make eyes, take two lengths of yarn B and tie a knot in each, winding yarn round four times to make the knots (see p. 122). Mark position of eyes on white stripe on head of zebra. Tie eyes to head and run ends into head. Embroider two nostrils in B, making two short stitches on muzzle two stitches apart (see p. 122 for beginning and fastening off embroidery invisibly).

RHINOS

Information you'll need

Finished size
Rhinos measure 4in (10cm) high

Materials
Any DK (US: light worsted) yarn
(NB: amounts are approximate)
50g grey (A)
Oddment of black for features
1 pair of 3.25mm (UK10:US3) needles and
1 spare needle the same size
Knitters' blunt-ended pins and a needle for
sewing up
Tweezers for stuffing small parts (optional)
Acrylic toy stuffing

Tension
26 sts x 34 rows to 4in (10cm) square over
st st using 3.25mm needles and DK yarn
before stuffing.

How to make Rhino

Legs and Body (make 2 pieces)

First leg

*Using the thumb method and A, cast on 6 sts.

Row 1 (WS): Purl.

Row 2: K1, m1, k4, m1, k1 (8 sts).

Beg with a p row, work 5 rows in st st.

Break yarn and set aside.

Second leg

Work as for first leg but do not break yarn.

Join legs

With RS facing, k across sts of second leg, turn and using the cable method cast on 12 sts, turn and with the same yarn cont knitting across sts of first leg (28 sts).

Beg with a p row, work 3 rows in st st. **

Place a marker on first and last sts of last row.

Work 12 rows in st st.

Next row: K2tog, k to last 2 sts, k2tog tbl (26 sts).

Next row: P2tog tbl, p to last 2 sts, p2tog (24 sts).

Rep last 2 rows twice (16 sts).

Cast off.

Legs and Gusset (make 2 pieces)

Work as for Legs and Body from * to **.

Cast off.

Head

Using the thumb method and A, cast on 14 sts.

Place a marker at centre of cast-on edge.

Row 1 (WS): Purl.

Row 2: K2, (m1, k1) 5 times, (k1, m1) 5 times, k2 (24 sts).

Beg with a p row, work 13 rows in st st.

Shape top of head

Row 16: (K2tog, k1) to end (16 sts).

Row 17: Purl.

Row 18: (K2tog) to end (8 sts).

Thread yarn through sts on needle, pull tight and secure by threading yarn a second time through sts.

Muzzle

Using the thumb method and A, cast on 22 sts.

Row 1 (WS): Purl.

Row 2: K5, k2tog, k8, k2tog, k5 (20 sts).

Beg with a p row, work 3 rows in st st.

Row 6: K4, k2tog, k8, k2tog, k4 (18 sts).

Beg with a p row, work 3 rows in st st.

Knit 2 rows for fold line.

Row 12: (K2tog, k1) to end (12 sts).

Row 13: Purl.

Row 14: (K2tog) to end (6 sts).

Thread yarn through sts on needle, pull tight and secure by threading yarn a second time through sts.

Horn

Using the thumb method and A, cast on 10 sts.

Beg with a p row, work 3 rows in st st.

Row 4 (RS): K2tog, k to last 2 sts, k2tog tbl (8 sts).

Row 5: Purl.

Rep last 2 rows twice (4 sts).

Thread yarn through sts on needle, pull tight and secure by threading yarn a second time through sts.

Ears (make 2)

Using the thumb method and A, cast on 6 sts.

Row 1 and foll alt row (WS): Purl.

Row 2: K2, m1, k2, m1, k2 (8 sts).

Row 4: K1, (k2tog) 3 times, k1 (5 sts).

Thread yarn through sts on needle, pull tight and secure by threading yarn a second time through sts.

Tail

Using the thumb method and A, cast on 6 sts.

Beg with a p row, work 5 rows in st st.

Row 6 (RS): K2, k2tog, k2 (5 sts).

Beg with a p row, work 3 rows in st st.

Thread yarn through sts on needle, pull tight and secure by threading yarn a second time through sts.

Making up

Body

Place right sides of body together, matching all edges. Sew around top edge from marker to marker. Do not remove markers yet. Turn right side out.

Legs and Gusset

With right sides together, place one set of legs and gusset on outside of one side of rhino, matching all edges. Sew around legs from marker to marker. Repeat for the other side. Turn legs right side out. Stuff each leg, then stuff the body and sew up the tummy seam.

Head and Muzzle

Join row ends of the head and stuff. Bring the seam and marker together and oversew the cast-on stitches. Join row ends of the muzzle and stuff. Sew cast-on stitches of muzzle to head, sewing lower edge of muzzle to lower edge of head all the way round. Pin and sew head to body.

Horn

Join row ends of horn by oversewing on the right side, sewing the seam tightly to curl the horn. Stuff the horn, pushing stuffing in with tweezers or tip of scissors. Sew cast-on stitches of horn to muzzle.

Ears

Join row ends of ears; with this seam at centre back, sew ears to head.

Tail

Join row ends of tail. Sew tail to rhino at back.

Features

To make eyes, take two lengths of black yarn and tie a knot in each, winding yarn round four times to make the knots (see p. 122). Mark position of eyes on rhino. Tie eyes to head and run ends into head.

SNAKES

Information you'll need

Finished size
Snakes measure 7in (18cm) long

Materials
Any DK (US: light worsted) yarn
(NB: amounts are approximate)
20g green (A)
10g dark green (B)
Oddments of gold and orange (C)
Oddments of red and black for features
1 pair of 3.25mm (UK10:US3) needles
Knitters' blunt-ended pins and a needle
for sewing up
Tweezers for stuffing small parts (optional)
Acrylic toy stuffing
2 pipe cleaners

Tension
26 sts x 34 rows to 4in (10cm) square over
st st using 3.25mm needles and DK yarn
before stuffing.

How to make Snake

Body

Divide A into 2 separate balls.

Beg at neck using the thumb method and A (first ball), cast on 11 sts.

Row 1 (WS): Purl.

Join on A (second ball) and B and work in st st in stripe, carrying the yarn loosely up sides of work. Join on gold or orange (C) and work a single st at centre, carrying yarn loosely up WS of centre, and work in patt as foll:

Row 1: Using B, k5, using C, k1, using B, k5.

Row 2: Using A, purl (second ball).

Row 3: Using A, knit.

Row 4: Using B, p5, using C, p1, using B, p5.

Row 5: Using A, knit.

Row 6: Using A, purl.

Rows 1–6 set the patt and are rep 5 times more.

Decrease for tail

Keeping patt correct as set throughout, dec as foll:

Next row: K2tog, k to last 2 sts, k2tog tbl (9 sts).

Work 5 rows in patt.

Rep last 6 rows twice more (5 sts).

Thread yarn through sts on needle, pull tight and secure by threading yarn a second time through sts.

Head

Beg at neck using the thumb method and A, cast on 11 sts.

Row 1 (WS): Purl.

Row 2: K3, (m1, k1) 6 times, k2 (17 sts).

Beg with a p row, work 5 rows in st st.

Row 8: K4, (k2tog) twice, k1, (k2tog) twice, k4 (13 sts).

Beg with a p row, work 3 rows in st st.

Row 12: K2, (k2tog) twice, k1, (k2tog) twice, k2 (9 sts).

Thread yarn through sts on needle and leave loose.

Making up

Tongue

Take a piece of red yarn approx. 10in (25cm) in length and tie two single tight knots at each end, approx. 1in (2cm) from the ends. Trim ends beyond knots close to knots. Fold yarn in half bringing knots together and tie a single overhand knot ½in (1.5cm) away from ends with knots. Trim folded ends to approx.1in (2cm). Insert single knot into centre of stitches on a thread of the head and pull these stitches tight. Sew through knot on wrong side of head to secure.

Head

Join row ends of head by oversewing on right side. Stuff head, pushing in stuffing with tweezers or tip of scissors, and leave cast-on stitches at neck open.

Body

Place a pipe cleaner along wrong side of body. Join row ends from tip of tail to neck using mattress stitch (see p. 121) on right side, pushing in a little stuffing with tweezers or tip of scissors as you sew. Sew cast-on stitches of body to cast-on stitches of head all the way round.

Features

To make eyes, take two lengths of black yarn and tie a knot in each, winding yarn round four times to make the knots (see p. 122). Mark position of eyes on snake. Tie eyes to head and run ends into head.

LITTLE MONKEYS

Information you'll need

Finished size
Monkeys measure 4in (10cm) high

Materials
Any DK (US: light worsted) yarn
(NB: amounts are approximate)
20g brown (A)
5g beige (B)
Oddment of black for features
1 pair of 3.25mm (UK10:US3) needles
Knitters' blunt-ended pins and a needle
for sewing up
Acrylic toy stuffing
10 pipe cleaners

Tension
26 sts x 34 rows to 4in (10cm) square
over st st using 3.25mm needles and
DK yarn before stuffing.

How to make Monkey

Body and Head
Beg at base using the thumb method and A, cast on 8 sts.
Row 1 and foll alt row (WS): Purl.
Row 2: (Inc 1) to end (16 sts).
Row 4: (Inc 1, k1) to end (24 sts).
Beg with a p row, work 5 rows in st st.
Row 10: (K2tog, k2) to end (18 sts).
Beg with a p row, work 5 rows in st st.
Row 16: (K2tog, k1) to end (12 sts).
Row 17: Purl.
Row 18: K3, (m1, k2) 4 times, k1 (16 sts).
Beg with a p row, work 9 rows in st st.
Row 28: (K2tog) to end (8 sts).
Thread yarn through sts on needle and leave loose.

Eye Piece
Using the thumb method and B, cast on 8 sts.
Row 1 (WS): Purl.
Thread yarn through sts on needle, pull tight and secure by threading yarn a second time through sts.

Muzzle
Using the thumb method and B, cast on 10 sts.
Row 1 (WS): Purl.
Row 2: (K1, k3tog, k1) twice (6 sts).
Thread yarn through sts on needle, pull tight and secure by threading yarn a second time through sts.

Ears (make 2)
Using the thumb method and B, cast on 5 sts.
Thread yarn through sts on needle, pull tight and secure by threading yarn a second time through sts.

Arms and Legs (make 4)
Using the thumb method and A, cast on 8 sts for WS facing for first row.
Beg with a p row, work 13 rows in st st.
Change to B and work 4 rows in st st.
Thread yarn through sts on needle, pull tight and secure by threading yarn a second time through sts.

Tail
Using the thumb method and A, cast on 6 sts for WS facing for first row.
Beg with a p row, work 25 rows in st st.
Thread yarn through sts on needle, pull tight and secure by threading yarn a second time through sts.

Making up

Body and Head
Gather round cast-on stitches, pull tight and secure. Join row ends of body and head. Stuff body, then lightly stuff head. Pull stitches on a thread tight at top of head and fasten off.

Eye Piece and Muzzle
Join row ends of muzzle and place a tiny ball of stuffing inside. Sew eye piece to head and sew muzzle to lower edge of eye piece and head all the way round.

Features
To make eyes, take two lengths of black yarn and tie a knot in each, winding yarn round three times to make the knots (see p. 122). Tie eyes to eye piece and run ends into head. Embroider nose and mouth in black using straight stitches as shown in picture above (see p. 122 for beginning and fastening off embroidery invisibly).

Ears
Sew ears to head at each side.

Arms and Legs
Take four pipe cleaners and fold each one in half. For each arm and leg, place folded end of pipe cleaner into wrong side of stitches pulled tight on a thread. Join row ends using mattress stitch (see p. 121) around pipe cleaner. Trim excess pipe cleaner and gather round cast-on stitches, pull tight and secure. Sew arms and legs to monkey and bend at knees and elbows.

Tail
Fold pipe cleaner in half and place folded end of pipe cleaner into wrong side of stitches pulled tight on a thread. Join row ends using mattress stitch around pipe cleaner. Trim excess pipe cleaner and sew tail to monkey at back. Bend tail.

TOUCANS

Information you'll need

Finished size
Toucans measure 3in (7.5cm) high

Materials
Any DK (US: light worsted) yarn
(NB: amounts are approximate)
15g black (A)
5g white (B)
5g orange (C)
5g gold (D)
Oddment of grey (E)
1 pair of 3.25mm (UK10:US3) needles
Knitters' blunt-ended pins and a needle
for sewing up
Tweezers for stuffing small parts (optional)
Acrylic toy stuffing

Tension
26 sts x 34 rows to 4in (10cm) square over
st st using 3.25mm needles and DK yarn
before stuffing.

How to make Toucan

Body and Head

Beg at base using the thumb method and A, cast on 14 sts.

Row 1 and foll alt row (WS): Purl.
Row 2: K2, (m1, k2) to end (20 sts).
Row 4: K5, (m1, k2) 6 times, k3 (26 sts).
Beg with a p row, work 5 rows in st st.
Row 10: K10, k2tog, k2, k2tog, k10 (24 sts).
Row 11 and foll alt row: Purl.
Row 12: K9, K2tog, k2, k2tog, k9 (22 sts).
Cut 2 pieces of B, each 48in (120cm) long.
Cut 2 pieces of C, each 40in (100cm) long.
Join on colours as needed and work in intarsia, twisting yarn when changing colour to avoid a hole.
Row 1: Using B, k2, using A, k6, k2tog, k2, k2tog, k6, using B (second piece), k2 (20 sts).
Row 2: Using B, p3, using A, p14, using B, p3.
Row 3: Using B, k4, using A, k3, k2tog, k2, k2tog, k3, using B, k4 (18 sts).
Rows 4, 6, 8 and 10: Using B, p4, using A, p10, using B, p4.
Rows 5, 7 and 9: Using B, k4, using A, k10, using B, k4.
Rows 11 and 13: Using C, k4, using A, k10, using C, k4.
Rows 12 and 14: Using C, p4, using A, p10, using C, p4.
Row 15: Using A, (k2tog) to end (9 sts).
Row 16: Using A, purl.
Thread yarn through sts on needle, pull tight and secure by threading yarn a second time through sts.

Beak

Cut 2 pieces of C, each 80in (200cm) long. Using the thumb method and one piece of C, cast on 3 sts, then onto the same needle and using D cast on 8 sts, then onto the same needle and using C (second piece) cast on 3 sts (14 sts).
Work in intarsia, twisting yarn when changing colour to avoid a hole.
Rows 1, 3 and 5 (WS): Using C, p3, using D, p8, using C, p3.
Rows 2 and 4: Using C, k3, using D, k8, using C, k3.
Row 6: Using C, k3, using D, k2, k2tog tbl, k2tog, k2, using C, k3 (12 sts).
Rows 7 and 9: Using C, p3, using D, p6, using C, p3.
Row 8: Using C, k3, using D, k6, using C, k3.
Row 10: Using C, k2, using D, k2tog, k4, k2tog tbl, using C, k2 (10 sts).
Rows 11 and 13: Using C, p2, using D, p6, using C, p2.
Row 12: Using C, k2, using D, k6, using C, k2.
Row 14: Using C, k2, using D, k1, k2tog tbl, k2tog, k1, using C, k2 (8 sts).
Row 15: Using C, p2, using D, p4, using C, p2.
Row 16: Using C, k2tog, using D, k2tog tbl, k2tog, using C, k2tog tbl (4 sts).
Thread yarn through sts on needle, pull tight and secure by threading yarn a second time through sts.

Tail

Beg at base using the thumb method and B, cast on 10 sts.
Row 1 and foll alt row (WS): Purl.
Row 2: K2, m1, k6, m1, k2 (12 sts).
Row 4: K3, m1, k6, m1, k3 (14 sts).
Row 5: Purl.
Change to A and work 2 rows in st st.
Row 8: K3, m1, k8, m1, k3 (16 sts).
Beg with a p row, work 3 rows in st st.
Cast off.

Wings (make 2)

Using the thumb method and A, cast on 8 sts.
Row 1 (WS): Purl.
Row 2: K1, m1, k6, m1, k1 (10 sts).
Beg with a p row, work 3 rows in st st.
Row 6: K2tog, k to last 2 sts, k2tog tbl (8 sts).
Row 7: Purl.
Rep last 2 rows twice (4 sts).
Thread yarn through sts on needle, pull tight and secure by threading yarn a second time through sts.

Feet (make 2)

Using the thumb method and E, cast on 6 sts for WS facing for first row.
Beg with a p row, work 3 rows in st st.
Cast off.

Making up

Body and Head

Weave in all loose ends around intarsia. Join row ends at centre front from top of head to lower edge using mattress stitch (see p. 121). Stuff head and body. Fold cast-on stitches in half and oversew.

Beak
Join row ends of beak, sewing tightly to curve beak. Stuff the beak, pushing the stuffing in with tweezers or tip of scissors. Sew cast-on stitches of beak to head at top.

Features
To make eyes, take two lengths of yarn A and tie a knot in each, winding yarn round three times to make the knots (see p. 122). Mark position of eyes on toucan. Tie eyes to head, one to each side and run ends into head. Embroider spot on each side of beak in A, as shown in picture above (see p. 122 for beginning and fastening off embroidery invisibly).

Tail
Join row ends of tail; with this seam at the centre of the underneath edge, oversew cast-on stitches and cast-off stitches. Sew tail to lower back, sewing all the way around the white part.

Wings
With right side of stocking-stitch outside, fold each wing and join row ends from tip to cast-on stitches and oversew cast-on stitches. Sew each wing to either side of toucan.

Feet
With right side of stocking-stitch outside, join cast-on and cast-off stitches of each foot. Fold each foot in half and join the seam at the lower edge. Place the toucan on a flat surface to position feet and sew in place.

CROCODILES

Information you'll need

Finished size
Crocodiles measure 8½in (21.5cm) long

Materials
Any DK (US: light worsted) yarn
(NB: amounts are approximate)
50g green (A)
Oddments of black and white for features
1 pair of 3.25mm (UK10:US3) needles
Knitters' blunt-ended pins and a needle
for sewing up
Tweezers for stuffing small parts (optional)
Acrylic toy stuffing

Tension
26 sts x 34 rows to 4in (10cm) square over
st st using 3.25mm needles and DK yarn
before stuffing.

How to make Crocodile

Tail, Body and Head

Beg at tail using the thumb method and A, cast on 5 sts.

Row 1 (WS): Purl.

Row 2: K1, (m1, k1) to end (9 sts).

Row 3: P3, k1, p1, k1, p3 (this row sets moss st).

Rows 4, 6, 8, 10, 12, 14: K4, p1, k4.

Rows 5, 7, 9, 11, 13, 15: P3, k1, p1, k1, p3.

Row 16: (K1, m1) twice, k1, moss st 3, k1, (m1, k1) twice (13 sts).

Rows 17, 19, 21, 23, 25, 27: P3, moss st 7, p3.

Rows 18, 20, 22, 24, 26: K3, moss st 7, k3.

Row 28: K2, m1, k1, m1, moss st 7, m1, k1, m1, k2 (17 sts).

Rows 29, 31, 33, 35, 37: P5, moss st 7, p5.

Rows 30, 32, 34, 36: K5, moss st 7, k5.

Row 38: K3, (m1, k1) twice, moss st 7, (k1, m1) twice, k3 (21 sts).

Rows 39, 41, 43, 45: P5, moss st 11, p5.

Rows 40, 42, 44: K5, moss st 11, k5.

Row 46: K4, m1, k1, m1, moss st 11, m1, k1, m1, k4 (25 sts).

Rows 47, 49, 51, 53, 55, 57: P7, moss st 11, p7.

Rows 48, 50, 52, 54, 56: K7, moss st 11, k7.

Row 58: K6, k3tog, moss st 7, k3tog, k6 (21 sts).

Row 59: P7, moss st 7, p7.

Row 60: K5, k2tog, moss st 7, k2tog, k5 (19 sts).

Work head

Beg with a p row, work 9 rows in st st.

Next row: K4, (k2tog, k1) 4 times, k3 (15 sts).

Next row: P4, p2tog, p3, p2tog, p4 (13 sts). Work 10 rows in st st.

Next row: K1, (k2tog, k1) to end (9 sts). Thread yarn through sts on needle, pull tight and secure by threading yarn a second time through sts.

Legs (make 4)

Using the thumb method and A, cast on 10 sts for WS facing for first row.
Beg with a p row, work 5 rows in st st.
Cast off.

Feet (make 4)

Using the thumb method and A, cast on 5 sts.
Beg with a p row, work 4 rows in st st, ending on a k row.

Row 5 (WS): K2tog, yf, k1, yf, k2tog tbl. Beg with a k row, work 4 rows in st st, ending on a k row.
Cast off.

Making up

Tail, Body and Head

Join row ends of head and stuff the head. Join row ends of tail and stuff, pushing the stuffing in with tweezers or tip of scissors. Join row ends of body, leaving a gap. Stuff lightly, keeping the body flat, and then close the gap.

Legs and Feet

With right side of stocking-stitch outside, roll each leg up from one set of row ends to the other and sew in place along the row ends of the outside edge. Sew a gathering stitch round the cast-on stitches, pull tight and secure. With right side of stocking-stitch outside, fold each foot along the shaped row. Join row ends and cast-on and cast-off stitches. Sew cast-off stitches of each leg to feet, positioning base edge of leg at back of foot. Place the crocodile on a flat surface to position legs and sew each leg to crocodile.

Features

To make eyes, take two lengths of black yarn and tie a knot in each, winding yarn round four times to make the knots (see p. 122). Mark position of eyes on crocodile. Tie eyes to head and run ends into head. Embroider the mouth in black using backstitch and teeth in white using straight stitches, as shown in picture on facing page (see p. 122 for beginning and fastening off embroidery invisibly).

PENGUINS

Information you'll need

Finished size
Penguins measure 3in (7.5cm) high

Materials
Any DK (US: light worsted) yarn
(NB: amounts are approximate)
20g black (A)
5g white (B)
5g yellow (C)
5g orange (D)
Oddment of grey for features
1 pair of 3.25mm (UK10:US3) needles
Knitters' blunt-ended pins and a needle
for sewing up
Acrylic toy stuffing

Tension
26 sts x 34 rows to 4in (10cm) square over
st st using 3.25mm needles and DK yarn
before stuffing.

How to make Penguin

Body and Head

Divide A into 2 separate balls.

Beg at lower edge using the thumb method and first ball of A, cast on 14 sts.

Row 1 (WS): Purl.

Row 2: K2, (m1, k2) to end (20 sts).

Join on B and second ball of A and work in intarsia, twisting yarn when changing colour to avoid a hole.

Row 3: Using A, p6, using B, p8, using A (second ball), p6.

Row 4: Using A, (k1, m1) twice, k4, using B, k8, using A, k4, (m1, k1) twice (24 sts).

Row 5: Using A, p8, using B, p8, using A, p8.

Row 6: Using A, (k1, m1) twice, k6, using B, k8, using A, k6, (m1, k1) twice (28 sts).

Rows 7 and 9: Using A, p10, using B, p8, using A, p10.

Row 8: Using A, k10, using B, k8, using A, k10.

Row 10: Using A, k2tog, k8, using B, k8, using A, k8, k2tog tbl (26 sts).

Row 11: Using A, p9, using B, p8, using A, p9.

Row 12: Using A, k2tog, k7, using B, k8, using A, k7, k2tog tbl (24 sts).

Row 13: Using A, p8, using B, p8, using A, p8.

Row 14: Using A, k2tog, k6, using B, k8, using A, k6, k2tog tbl (22 sts).

Row 15: Using A, p7, using B, p8, using A, p7.

Row 16: Using A, k2tog, k5, using B, k8, using A, k5, k2tog tbl (20 sts).

Rows 17 and 19: Using A, p6, using B, p8, using A, p6.

Row 18: Using A, k6, using B, k8, using A, k6.

Row 20: (Break off B and join on C), using A, k6, using C, k2tog tbl, k4, k2tog, using A, k6 (18 sts).

Row 21: Using A, p6, using C, p6, using A, p6.

Row 22: Using A, k6, using C, k6, using A, k6.

Cont with 1 ball of A and beg with a p row, work 7 rows in st st.

Row 30: (K2tog, k1) to end (12 sts).

Row 31: Purl.

Row 32: (K2tog) to end (6 sts).

Thread yarn through sts on needle, pull tight and secure by threading yarn a second time through sts.

Feet (make 2)

Using the thumb method and D, cast on 4 sts for WS facing for first row.

Beg with a p row, work 5 rows in st st.

Cast off.

Flippers (make 2)

Using the thumb method and A, cast on 5 sts.

Row 1 (WS): Purl.

Row 2: K1, (m1, k1) to end (9 sts).

Beg with a p row, work 5 rows in st st.

Row 8: K2, k2tog, k1, k2tog, k2 (7 sts).

Row 9 and foll alt row: Purl.

Row 10: K1, (k2tog, k1) twice (5 sts).

Row 12: K2tog, k1, k2tog tbl (3 sts).

Thread yarn through sts on needle, pull tight and secure by threading yarn a second time through sts.

Beak

Using the thumb method and D, cast on 6 sts.

Row 1 (WS): Purl.

Row 2: K1, (k2tog) twice, k1 (4 sts).

Thread yarn through sts on needle, pull tight and secure by threading yarn a second time through sts.

Making up

Body and Head

Weave in ends around intarsia. Join row ends of body and head and then stuff, pushing stuffing into head and tail. Gather round cast-on stitches, pull tight and secure.

Feet

Join cast-on and cast-off stitches of each foot. Place penguin on a flat surface, position feet and sew in place.

Flippers

Join row ends of each flipper and sew to penguin at each side.

Beak

Join row ends of beak and sew cast-on stitches to head at centre front.

Features

To make eyes, take two pieces of grey yarn and tie a knot in each, winding yarn round three times to make the knots (see p. 122). Mark position of eyes on penguin. Tie eyes to head and run ends into head.

GIANT TORTOISES

Information you'll need

Finished size
Giant tortoises measure 3in (7.5cm) long

Materials
Any DK (US: light worsted) yarn
(NB: amounts are approximate)
10g khaki green (A)
10g green (B)
Oddment of black for features
1 pair of 3.25mm (UK10:US3) needles
Knitters' blunt-ended pins and a needle
for sewing up
Tweezers for stuffing small parts (optional)
Acrylic toy stuffing

Tension
26 sts x 34 rows to 4in (10cm) square over
st st using 3.25mm needles and DK yarn
before stuffing.

How to make Giant Tortoise
Shell
Beg at lower edge using the thumb method and A, cast on 43 sts and beg in garter st. Work 2 rows in garter st.
Join on B and carrying yarn loosely up side of work, work in patt as foll:
Row 1 (RS): Using B, k3, s1p, (k5, s1p) to last 3 sts, k3.
Row 2: Using B, p3, s1p, (p5, s1p) to last 3 sts, p3.
Rows 3 and 4: As rows 1 and 2.
Row 5: Using A, (k1, k2tog) to last st, k1 (29 sts).
Row 6: Using A, knit.
Row 7: Using B, k2, s1p, (k3, s1p) to last 2 sts, k2.
Row 8: Using B, p2, s1p, (p3, s1p) to last 2 sts, p2.
Rows 9 and 10: As rows 7 and 8.
Row 11: Using A, k1, (k2tog, k2) to end (22 sts).

Row 12: Using A, knit.
Row 13: *Using B, (k2tog) twice, k3, (k2tog) twice, rep from * once (14 sts).
Row 14: Using B, purl.
Row 15: Using B, (k2tog) to end (7 sts).
Thread yarn through sts on needle, pull tight and secure by threading yarn a second time through sts.

Base
Using the thumb method and A, cast on 5 sts.
Row 1 (WS): Purl.
Row 2: K next row and inc k-wise into first and last st (7 sts).
Row 3: P next row and inc p-wise into first and last st (9 sts).
Rep last 2 rows once (13 sts).
Work 12 rows in st st.
Row 18: K2tog, k to last 2 sts, k2tog

tbl (11 sts).
Row 19: P2tog tbl, p to last 2 sts, p2tog (9 sts).
Rep last 2 rows once (5 sts).
Cast off.

Legs (make 4)
Using the thumb method and A, cast on 8 sts for WS facing for first row.
Beg with a p row, work 5 rows in st st.
Thread yarn through sts on needle, pull tight and secure by threading yarn a second time through sts.

Head
Beg at lower edge using the thumb method and B, cast on 12 sts.
Beg with a p row, work 9 rows in st st.
Row 10 (RS): (K2tog) to end (6 sts).

Thread yarn through sts on needle, pull tight and secure by threading yarn a second time through sts.

Making up
Shell and Base
Join row ends of shell and stuff. Sew base to underneath of shell inside garter-stitch border at lower edge.

Legs
Join row ends of legs and stuff each leg, pushing stuffing in with tweezers or tip of scissors. With the seam at the centre of the underneath edge, sew across cast-on stitches. Sew cast-on stitches of each leg to underneath of tortoise.

Head
Join row ends of head and stuff. With the seam at the centre of the lower edge, sew across cast-on stitches. Sew cast-on stitches to underneath of tortoise, point head upwards and sew back of neck to shell.

Features
To make eyes, take two pieces of black yarn and tie a knot in each, winding yarn round three times to make the knots (see p. 122). Mark position of eyes on tortoise. Tie eyes to head and run ends into head.

SHEEP

Information you'll need

Finished size
Sheep measure 3¼in (8cm) high

Materials
Any DK (US: light worsted) yarn
(NB: amounts are approximate)
30g golden cream (A)
5g fawn (B)
Oddment of black for features
1 pair of 3.25mm (UK10:US3) needles
Knitters' blunt-ended pins and a needle
for sewing up
Tweezers for stuffing small parts (optional)
Acrylic toy stuffing

Tension
26 sts x 34 rows to 4in (10cm) square over
st st using 3.25mm needles and DK yarn
before stuffing.

How to make Ram

Body

Beg at lower edge using the thumb method and A, cast on 18 sts and work in garter st.

Work 2 rows in garter st.

Row 3 (RS): (K1, m1, k1, m1, k5, m1, k1, m1, k1) twice (26 sts).

Row 4: Knit.

Row 5: (K1, m1, k2, m1, k7, m1, k2, m1, k1) twice (34 sts).

Work 15 rows in garter st.

Row 21: (K2tog) twice, k9, (k2tog) 4 times, k9, (k2tog) twice (26 sts).

Work 3 rows in garter st.

Row 25: (K2tog) twice, k5, (k2tog) 4 times, k5, (k2tog) twice (18 sts).

Cast off in garter st.

Legs (make 4)

Beg at lower edge using the thumb method and A, cast on 8 sts.

Row 1 (WS): Purl.

Row 2: K2, (m1, k2) to end (11 sts).

Beg with a p row, work 5 rows in st st.

Cast off 3 sts at beg of next 2 rows (5 sts).

Row 10: K2tog, k1, k2tog tbl (3 sts).

Cast off p-wise.

Head

Beg at centre back using the thumb method and A, cast on 6 sts and beg in garter st.

Row 1 (RS): (Inc 1 k-wise) to end (12 sts).

Row 2 and foll alt row: Knit.

Row 3: (Inc 1, k1) to end (18 sts).

Row 5: (Inc 1, k2) to end (24 sts).

Work 5 rows in garter st.

Cont in st st and dec.

Row 11: (K2tog, k2) to end (18 sts).

Beg with a p row, work 3 rows in st st.

Row 15: (K2tog, k1) to end (12 sts).

Beg with a p row, work 3 rows in st st.

Row 19: (K2tog) to end (6 sts).

Thread yarn through sts on needle, pull tight and secure by threading yarn a second time through sts.

Ears (make 2)

Using the thumb method and A, cast on 10 sts.

Row 1 (RS): K3, (k2tog) twice, k3 (8 sts).

Cast off k-wise.

Horns (make 2)

Beg at base edge using the thumb method and B, cast on 8 sts.

Beg with a p row, work 3 rows in st st.

Shape horn

Row 1 (RS): K6, turn.

Row 2: S1p, p3, turn.

Row 3: S1k, k to end.

Row 4: Purl.

Rep rows 1–4 once.

Row 9: K2tog, k4, k2tog tbl (6 sts).

Row 10: Purl.

Row 11: K2tog, k2, k2tog tbl (4 sts).

Thread yarn through sts on needle, pull tight and secure by threading yarn a second time through sts.

Tail

Using the thumb method and A, cast on 6 sts and work in garter st.

Work 2 rows in garter st.

Row 3 (RS): (K2tog) twice, inc into last 2 sts.

Work 5 rows in garter st.

Row 9: Inc into first 2 sts, k2tog, k2tog tbl.

Work 3 rows in garter st.

Thread yarn through sts on needle, pull tight and secure by threading yarn a second time through sts.

Making up

Body

Fold cast-off stitches of body in half and oversew. Join row ends of body and stuff. Fold cast-on stitches in half and oversew.

Legs

Fold cast-on stitches of legs in half and oversew. Join straight row ends of legs and stuff, pushing stuffing in with tweezers or tip of scissors. Sew legs to body.

Head

Gather round cast-on stitches of head, pull tight and secure. Join row ends, leaving a gap, stuff, and close the gap. Pin and sew head to body.

Ears

Fold cast-off stitches of ears in half and oversew. Fold row ends in half and catch in place. Sew ears to head at each side.

Horns

Join row ends of horns, sewing tightly to curl horns. Stuff, pushing stuffing in with tweezers or tip of scissors. Sew cast-on stitches of horns to head behind ears and curl horns round and catch tip of horns in place.

Tail

Join row ends of tail and sew cast-on stitches to body.

Features

To make eyes, take two lengths of black yarn and tie a knot in each, winding yarn round three times to make the knots (see p. 122). Tie eyes to head with three clear knitted stitches in between and run ends into head. Embroider nose and mouth in black using straight stitches (see p. 122 for beginning and fastening off embroidery invisibly).

How to make Ewe

Make Body, Legs, Head, Ears and Tail
in A as for ram.

Making up

Make up as for ram, omitting horns.

PIGS

Information you'll need

Finished size
Pigs measure 3¼in (8cm) high

Materials
Any DK (US: light worsted) yarn
(NB: amounts are approximate)
30g pink (A)
Oddment of black for features
1 pair of 3.25mm (UK10:US3) needles
Knitters' blunt-ended pins and a needle
for sewing up
Acrylic toy stuffing

Tension
26 sts x 34 rows to 4in (10cm) square over
st st using 3.25mm needles and DK yarn
before stuffing.

How to make Pig

Legs and Body (make 2 pieces)

First leg
*Using the thumb method and A, cast on 4 sts.
Row 1 (WS): Purl.
Row 2: K1, m1, k2, m1, k1 (6 sts).
Beg with a p row, work 3 rows in st st.
Break yarn and set aside.

Second leg
Work as for first leg but do not break yarn.

Join legs
With RS facing, k across sts of second leg, turn and using the cable method cast on 8 sts, turn and with the same yarn cont knitting across sts of first leg (20 sts).
Purl 1 row then knit 1 row. **
Place marker on first and last sts of last row.
Beg with a p row, work 11 rows in st st.
Next row: K2tog, k to last 2 sts, k2tog tbl (18 sts).
Next row: P2tog tbl, p to last 2 sts, p2tog (16 sts).
Rep last 2 rows once (12 sts).
Cast off.

Legs and Gusset (make 2 pieces)
Work as for Legs and Body from * to **.
Cast off p-wise.

Head
Beg at lower edge using the thumb method and A, cast on 14 sts.
Row 1 and foll alt row (WS): Purl.
Row 2: (K3, m1, k1, m1, k3) twice (18 sts).
Row 4: (K4, m1, k1, m1, k4) twice (22 sts).
Beg with a p row, work 9 rows in st st.
Row 14: (K3, k2tog, k1, k2tog, k3) twice (18 sts).
Row 15 and foll alt row: Purl.
Row 16: (K2, k2tog, k1, k2tog, k2) twice (14 sts).

Row 18: (K1, k2tog, k1, k2tog, k1) twice (10 sts).
Row 19: (P2tog) to end (5 sts).
Thread yarn through sts on needle, pull tight and secure by threading yarn a second time through sts.

Snout
Using the thumb method and A, cast on 12 sts.
Row 1 (WS): Purl.
Knit 2 rows for fold line.
Row 4: (K2tog, k1) to end (8 sts).
Thread yarn through sts on needle, pull tight and secure by threading yarn a second time through sts.

Ears (make 2)
Beg at base edge using the thumb method and A, cast on 9 sts.
Beg with a p row, work 3 rows in st st.
Row 4 (RS): (K2tog) twice, k1, k2tog, k2tog tbl (5 sts).
Row 5: Purl.
Row 6: K2tog, k1, k2tog tbl (3 sts).
Thread yarn through sts on needle, pull tight and secure by threading yarn a second time through sts.

Making up

Tail
Make a twisted cord out of four strands of yarn, each 24in (60cm) long (see p. 123). Tie a tight knot 2in (5cm) from folded end and tie another knot for external tail at folded end. Trim ends beyond tight knot to ½in (1cm).

Body
Place right sides of body together, matching all edges. Sew around top edge from marker to marker; enclose the tail in this seam halfway between the marker and the beginning of the shaped row ends. Sew tail in place securely; the tight knot will be on the wrong side. Do not remove markers yet. Turn right side out.

Legs and Gusset
With right sides together, place one set of legs and gusset on outside of one side of pig, matching all edges. Sew around legs from marker to marker. Repeat for the other side. Turn legs right side out. Place a small ball of stuffing into each leg, then stuff the body and sew up the tummy seam.

Head
Join row ends and stuff; with this seam at centre back, oversew the cast-on stitches.

Snout
Join row ends of snout and stuff with a small ball of stuffing. Sew snout to lower half of head all the way round.

Ears
Join row ends of ears; with this seam at centre of inside edge, sew cast-on stitches of ears to each side of head. Curl ears forwards and catch in place.

Features
To make eyes, take two lengths of black yarn and tie a knot in each, winding yarn round three times to make the knots (see p. 122). Tie eyes to head on second row above snout with three clear knitted stitches in between and run ends into head. Pin and sew head to pig.

CHICKENS

Information you'll need

Finished size
Chickens measure 2in (5cm) high

Materials
Any DK (US: light worsted) yarn
(NB: amounts are approximate)
10g fawn (A)
5g yellow (B)
5g red (C)
5g petrol blue (D)
5g jade (E)
10g ginger (F)
Oddment of black for features
1 pair of 3.25mm (UK10:US3) needles
Knitters' blunt-ended pins and a needle
for sewing up
Acrylic toy stuffing

Tension
26 sts x 34 rows to 4in (10cm) square over
st st using 3.25mm needles and DK yarn
before stuffing.

How to make Cockerel

Body and Head

Begin at lower edge using the thumb method and A, cast on 10 sts.

Row 1 and foll 4 alt rows (WS): Purl.

Row 2: (K1, m1, k3, m1, k1) twice (14 sts).

Row 4: (K1, m1, k5, m1, k1) twice (18 sts).

Row 6: (K1, m1, k7, m1, k1) twice (22 sts).

Row 8: (K1, m1, k9, m1, k1) twice (26 sts).

Row 10: (K1, m1, k11, m1, k1) twice (30 sts).

Row 11: Purl.

Shape tail

Row 12: K5, turn.

Row 13: S1p, p to end.

Row 14: K3, turn.

Row 15: S1p, p to end.

Row 16: Knit.

Row 17: P5, turn.

Row 18: S1k, k to end.

Row 19: P3, turn.

Row 20: S1k, k to end.

Row 21: Purl.

Cast off 8 sts at beg of next 2 rows (14 sts).

Next row: k2tog, k to last 2 sts, k2tog tbl (12 sts).

Beg with a p row, work 3 rows in st st.

Next row: (k2tog) to end (6 sts).

Thread yarn through sts on needle, pull tight and secure by threading yarn a second time through sts.

Feet (make 2)

Using the thumb method and B, cast on 4 sts for WS facing for first row.

Beg with a p row, work 5 rows in st st.

Cast off k-wise.

Comb

Using the thumb method and C, cast on 6 sts.

Thread yarn through sts on needle, pull tight and secure by threading yarn a second time through sts.

Beak

Using the thumb method and B, cast on 6 sts.

Row 1 (WS): P2tog tbl, (p2tog) twice (3 sts).

Thread yarn through sts on needle, pull tight and secure by threading yarn a second time through sts.

Crop

Using the thumb method and C, cast on 8 sts.

Cast off k-wise.

Eye Pieces (make 2)

Using the thumb method and C, cast on 8 sts.

Row 1 (WS): P2, (p2tog) twice, p2 (6 sts).

Row 2: K1, (k2tog) twice, k1 (4 sts).

Thread yarn through sts on needle, pull tight and secure by threading yarn a second time through sts.

Wings (make 2)

Using the thumb method and A, cast on 4 sts.

Row 1 (WS): Inc p-wise into every st (8 sts).

Beg with a k row, work 4 rows in st st.

Row 6: K2tog, k to last 2 sts, k2tog tbl (6 sts).

Row 7: Purl.

Rep dec row once (4 sts).

Thread yarn through sts on needle, pull tight and secure by threading yarn a second time through sts.

Tail

First piece

Using the cable method and D, cast on 10 sts.

*__Row 1:__ Cast off 7 sts k-wise at beg of row and k to end (3 sts).

Row 2: Knit.

Using the cable method, cast on 7 sts (10 sts).

Rep from * once.

Cast off all sts.

Second piece

Using the cable method and E, cast on 13 sts.

**__Row 1:__ Cast off 10 sts k-wise at beg of row and k to end (3 sts).

Row 2: Knit.

Using the cable method, cast on 10 sts (13 sts).

Rep from ** twice.

Cast off all sts.

Making up

Body and Head

Join row ends of body and head and cast-off stitches at back. Stuff body, pushing stuffing into the head and tail. Fold cast-on stitches in half and oversew.

Feet

Join cast-on and cast-off stitches of feet. Place cockerel on a flat surface, position the feet and sew in place.

Comb, Beak and Crop

Sew comb to top of head all the way round lower edge. Sew beak to head all the way round. Fold crop in half and sew below beak.

Eye Pieces

Sew eye pieces to head around outside edge.

Wings

Fold wings in half and oversew row ends. Sew to sides of cockerel.

Tail

Gather round straight row ends of first piece of tail and sew to cockerel. Sew straight row ends of second piece of tail behind first piece.

Features

To make eyes, take two lengths of black yarn and tie a knot in each, winding yarn round three times to make the knots (see p. 122). Tie eyes to eye pieces and run ends into head.

How to make Hen

Make Body, Head and Wings in F as for cockerel. Make Feet, Comb, Beak, Crop and Eye Pieces as for cockerel.

Making up

Make up as for cockerel, omitting tail.

OWLS

Information you'll need

Finished size
Owls measure 2¼in (6cm) high

Materials
Any DK (US: light worsted) yarn
(NB: amounts are approximate)
10g brown (A)
5g mustard (B)
5g oatmeal (C)
5g grey (D)
Oddment of black for features
1 pair of 3.25mm (UK10:US3) needles
Knitters' blunt-ended pins and a needle
for sewing up
Acrylic toy stuffing

Tension
26 sts x 34 rows to 4in (10cm) square over
st st using 3.25mm needles and DK yarn
before stuffing.

How to make Owl

Back and Front (make 2 pieces)

Beg at lower edge using the thumb method and A, cast on 7 sts.

Row 1 (WS): Purl.

Row 2: (K1, m1) twice, k3, (m1, k1) twice (11 sts).

Beg with a p row, work 9 rows in st st.

Row 12: K2tog, k to last 2 sts, k2tog tbl (9 sts).

Beg with a p row, work 7 rows in st st.

Shape ears

Row 20: (K1, m1) twice, k5, (m1, k1) twice (13 sts).

Row 21: Purl.

Cast off.

Tummy

Beg at lower edge using the thumb method and B, cast on 7 sts and work in moss st.

Row 1 (RS): K1, (p1, k1) to end.

Row 2: (Inc 1 k-wise) twice, k1, p1, (inc 1 k-wise) twice, k1 (11 sts).

Row 3: K1, (p1, k1) to end.

Row 4: (Inc 1 k-wise) twice, (k1, p1) 3 times, (inc 1 k-wise) twice, k1 (15 sts).

Row 5: K1, (p1, k1) to end.

Rep last row 5 times more.

Row 11: K1, p3tog, k1, (p1, k1) 3 times, p3tog, k1 (11 sts).

Row 12: K1, (p1, k1) to end.

Row 13: K1, p3tog, k1, p1, k1, p3tog, k1 (7 sts).

Cast off in k1, p1 moss st.

Eye Pieces (make 2)

Using the thumb method and C, cast on 14 sts.

Row 1 (RS): (K2tog) to end (7 sts).

Thread yarn through sts on needle, pull tight and secure by threading yarn a second time through sts.

Beak

Using the thumb method and D, cast on 5 sts.

Thread yarn through sts on needle, pull tight and secure by threading yarn a second time through sts.

Wings (make 2)

Beg at top edge using the thumb method and A, cast on 6 sts.

Row 1 and foll alt row (WS): Purl.

Row 2: K1, (m1, k1) to end (11 sts).

Row 4: K5, m1, k1, m1, k5 (13 sts).

Beg with a p row, work 3 rows in st st.

Row 8: K1, (k2tog, k1) to end (9 sts).

Row 9: Purl.

Row 10: (K2tog) twice, k1, k2tog, k2tog tbl (5 sts).

Thread yarn through sts on needle, pull tight and secure by threading yarn a second time through sts.

Feet (make 2)

Using D, cast on 5 sts for WS facing for first row.

Purl 1 row then knit 1 row.

Cast off p-wise.

Tail

Using the thumb method and A, cast on 16 sts.

Beg with a p row, work 3 rows in st st.

Row 4 (RS): K3, k2tog, k6, k2tog, k3 (14 sts).

Row 5: Purl.

Row 6: K2, k2tog, k6, k2tog, k2 (12 sts).

Cast off p-wise.

Making up

Back and Front

Place right sides of back and front together, matching all edges. Join row ends and cast-off stitches at top. Turn right side out and stuff. Join lower edge.

Tummy

Place tummy on lower half of front of owl and sew cast-on stitches of both pieces together and all around outside edge of tummy.

Eye Pieces

Place eyes on head and sew around outside edge.

Beak

Sew beak to owl between eyes.

Wings

Join row ends of wings and sew wings to sides of owl.

Feet

Join cast-on and cast-off stitches of each foot and fold in half and catch in place. Place owl on a flat surface and position the feet. Sew in place.

Tail

Join row ends of tail; with this seam at the centre of the underneath edge, join cast-on then cast-off stitches. Sew tail to owl at back.

Features

To make eyes, take two lengths of black yarn and tie a knot in each, winding yarn round three times to make the knots (see p. 122). Tie to centre of eyes and run ends into head.

RAVEN & DOVE

Information you'll need

Finished size

Raven measures 2in (5cm) high
Dove measures 1½in (4cm) high

Materials

Any DK (US: light worsted) yarn
(NB: amounts are approximate)
10g black (A)
10g white (B)
Oddments of green (C) and grey
1 pair of 3.25mm (UK10:US3) needles
Knitters' blunt-ended pins and a needle
for sewing up
Tweezers for stuffing small parts (optional)
Acrylic toy stuffing

Tension

26 sts x 34 rows to 4in (10cm) square over
st st using 3.25mm needles and DK yarn
before stuffing.

Making up

Body, Head and Tail

Join row ends of body, head and tail by oversewing on right side, leaving a gap in middle. Stuff the tail, pushing the stuffing into the tail with tweezers or tip of scissors. Stuff head and body lightly, keeping flat, then close the gap.

Beak

Join row ends of cast-on stitches of beak and sew beak to front of head.

Wings

Join row ends of each wing; with this seam at the centre of the inside edge, sew wings to sides of raven.

Claws

Join cast-on and cast-off stitches of claws. Fold in half and sew to lower edge of raven.

Features

To make eyes, take two lengths of grey yarn and tie a knot in each, winding yarn round three times to make the knots (see p. 122). Mark position of eyes on raven. Tie eyes to head, one to each side, and run ends into head.

How to make Raven

Body, Head and Tail

Beg at tail using the thumb method and A, cast on 10 sts.

Beg with a p row, work 3 rows in st st.

Row 4 (RS): K2tog, k6, k2tog tbl (8 sts).

Beg with a p row, work 3 rows in st st.

Row 8: (K1, m1) twice, k4, (m1, k1) twice (12 sts).

Row 9: Purl.

Row 10: (K1, m1) twice, k8, (m1, k1) twice (16 sts).

Beg with a p row, work 7 rows in st st.

Row 18: (K2tog) twice, k3, m1, k2, m1, k3, k2tog, k2tog tbl (14 sts).

Row 19: P2tog tbl, p to last 2 sts, p2tog (12 sts).

Row 20: (K2tog) twice, k1, m1, k2, m1, k1, k2tog, k2tog tbl (10 sts).

Row 21 and foll alt row: Purl.

Row 22: (K1, m1) twice, k to last 2 sts, (m1, k1) twice (14 sts).

Row 24: (K2tog) to end (7 sts).

Thread yarn through sts on needle, pull tight and secure by threading yarn a second time through sts.

Beak

Using the thumb method and A, cast on 8 sts.

Thread yarn through sts on needle, pull tight and secure by threading yarn a second time through sts.

Wings (make 2)

Using the thumb method and A, cast on 6 sts.

Row 1 and foll alt row (WS): Purl.

Row 2: K1, m1, k4, m1, k1 (8 sts).

Row 4: K2tog, k to last 2 sts, k2tog tbl (6 sts).

Rep last 2 rows once (4 sts).

Thread yarn through sts on needle, pull tight and secure by threading yarn a second time through sts.

Claws

Using A, cast on 4 sts.

Cast off p-wise.

How to make Dove

Body and Head
Beg at back edge using the thumb method and B, cast on 10 sts.
Row 1 (WS): Purl.
Row 2: K1, m1, k to last st, m1, k1 (12 sts).
Rep first 2 rows twice (16 sts).
Beg with a p row, work 3 rows in st st.
Row 10: (K2tog) twice, k3, m1, k2, m1, k3, k2tog, k2tog tbl (14 sts).
Row 11 and foll alt row: Purl.
Row 12: K2tog, k4, m1, k2, m1, k4, k2tog tbl.
Row 14: (K2tog) to last 2 sts, k2tog tbl (7 sts).
Thread yarn through sts on needle, pull tight and secure by threading yarn a second time through sts.

Tail
Using the thumb method and B, cast on 5 sts.
Row 1 (WS): Purl.
Row 2: K1, (m1, k1) to end (9 sts).
Rep first 2 rows once (17 sts).
Row 5: Purl.
Row 6: Knit.
Picot edge: K1, (yf, k2tog) to end.
Row 8: Knit.
Row 9 and foll alt row: Purl.
Row 10: K2tog, (k1, k2tog) to end (11 sts).
Row 12: As row 10 (7 sts).
Cast off p-wise.

Leaf
Using the thumb method and C, cast on 6 sts.
Cast off p-wise.

Beak
Using the thumb method and B, cast on 6 sts.
Thread yarn through sts on needle, pull tight and secure by threading yarn a second time through sts.

Wings (make 2)
Using the thumb method and B, cast on 6 sts.
Row 1 and foll alt row (WS): Purl.
Row 2: K1, m1, k4, m1, k1 (8 sts).
Row 4: K2tog, k to last 2 sts, k2tog tbl (6 sts).
Rep last 2 rows once (4 sts).
Thread yarn through sts on needle, pull tight and secure by threading yarn a second time through sts.

Making up
Body and Head
Join row ends of body and head by oversewing on right side. Stuff head and body lightly, keeping flat and pushing the stuffing in with tweezers or tip of scissors. Fold cast-on stitches in half and join.

Tail
Join cast-on and cast-off stitches of tail; curve tail round and sew to back of dove.

Beak and Leaf
Join cast-on and cast-off stitches of lower half of leaf. Join row ends of cast-on stitches of beak and attach a leaf to tip. Sew beak to front of dove.

Wings
Join row ends of each wing; with this seam at the centre of the inside edge, sew wings to sides of dove.

Features
Embroider eyes in A, one on each side of head, making a small stitch over half a stitch (see p. 122 for starting and fastening off embroidery invisibly).

MR & MRS NOAH

Information you'll need

Finished size
Figures stand 4½in (11.5cm) high

Materials
Any DK (US: light worsted) yarn
(NB: amounts are approximate)
10g claret (A)
5g pink (flesh) (B)
10g dark green (C)
5g white (D)
10g purple (E)
5g blue (F)
Oddments of black, red and brown
1 pair of 3.25mm (UK10:US3) needles

Knitters' blunt-ended pins and a needle
for sewing up
Acrylic toy stuffing
Red pencil for shading cheeks

Tension
26 sts x 34 rows to 4in (10cm) square
over st st using 3.25mm needles and
DK yarn before stuffing.

How to make Noah

Body and Head

Beg at lower edge using the thumb method and A, cast on 16 sts.

Row 1 (WS): Purl.

Row 2: (K1, m1, k1) to end (24 sts).

Beg with a p row, work 15 rows in st st.

Row 18: (K3, k2tog, k2, k2tog, k3) twice (20 sts).

Beg with a p row, work 5 rows in st st.

Row 24: (K2, k2tog, k2, k2tog, k2) twice (16 sts).

Row 25: Purl.

Change to B for head and work 12 rows in st st.

Next row: (K2tog) to end (8 sts).

Thread yarn through sts on needle, pull tight and secure by threading yarn a second time through sts.

Base

Using the thumb method and A, cast on 16 sts.

Row 1 (WS): Purl.

Row 2: (K2tog) to end (8 sts).

Thread yarn through sts on needle, pull tight and secure by threading yarn a second time through sts.

Arms (make 2)

Beg at shoulder using the thumb method and A, cast on 10 sts.

Beg with a p row, work 9 rows in st st. Change to B for hand and work 2 rows in st st.

Row 12 (RS): (K2tog) to end (5 sts).

Thread yarn through sts on needle and leave loose.

Outer Garment

Beg at back using the thumb method and C, cast on 10 sts and work in garter st.

Work 26 rows in garter st.

Row 27 (RS): K3, k2tog tbl, turn.

Row 28: K4, turn and work on these 4 sts. Work 4 rows in garter st.

Row 33: K3, m1, k1 (5 sts).

Work 26 rows in garter st ending with a RS facing row.

Cast off in garter st.

Rejoin yarn to rem sts and dec.

Next row: K2tog, k3 (4 sts).

Work 5 rows in garter st.

Next row: K1, m1, k3 (5 sts).

Work 26 rows in garter st with a RS facing row.

Cast off in garter st.

Beard

Using the thumb method and D, cast on 9 sts and work in rev st st.

Row 1 (RS): Purl.

Row 2: K1, (m1, k1) to end (17 sts).

Row 3: P2tog tbl, p2tog, p8, turn.

Row 4: S1k, k6, turn.

Row 5: S1p, p to last 4 sts, (p2tog) twice (13 sts).

Row 6: (K2tog) twice, k5, k2tog, k2tog tbl (9 sts).

Row 7: P7, turn.

Row 8: S1k, k4, turn,

Row 9: S1p, p to end.

Row 10: (K1, m1) twice, k5, (m1, k1) twice (13 sts).

Row 11: Purl.

Row 12: (K1, m1) twice, k9, (m1, k1) twice (17 sts).

Row 13: P1, (p2tog) 3 times, p3, (p2tog) 3 times, p1 (11 sts).

Cast off k-wise.

Hair

Using the thumb method and D, cast on 20 sts for RS facing for first row.

Row 1: Purl.

Cast off k-wise.

Making up

Body, Head and Base

Join row ends of head and body, and stuff. Sew base to lower edge all the way round. To shape neck, take a double length of yarn to match body and sew a running stitch round last row of body, sewing in and out of every half stitch. Pull tight and knot yarn, sewing ends into neck.

Arms

Roll arms up from row ends to row ends and catch in place. Pull stitches on a thread tight and secure. Gather round stitches at shoulders, pull tight and secure. Sew arms to doll.

Outer Garment and Belt

Weave in all loose ends of outer garment and place on doll. To make belt, take one strand of brown, 35in (90cm) in length, and make a twisted cord (see p. 123). Tie belt around middle of doll using a double knot. Knot ends 1in (2.5cm) from waist and trim ends close to these knots.

Features

To make eyes, take two lengths of black yarn and tie a knot in each, winding yarn round three times to make the knots (see p. 122). Mark position of eyes on doll, on 7th row above neck with two clear knitted stitches in between. Tie eyes to head and run ends into head. Work nose in B, making a bundle of five short stitches over one stitch on row below eyes (see p. 122 for beginning and fastening off embroidery invisibly). Shade cheeks with a red pencil.

Beard and Hair

With reverse stocking-stitch outside, bring cast-on and cast-off stitches of beard together and join. Sew beard around face. Sew hair around head, attaching to sides of beard and pulling down to neck at back.

How to make Noah's wife

Make Body and Head, Base and Arms in E as for Noah.

Headdress

Top of headdress

Beg at lower edge using the thumb method and F, cast on 20 sts.
Join on E and purl 2 rows.
Cont in F and beg with a p row, work 3 rows in st st.
Row 6 (RS): (K2tog, k2) to end (15 sts).
Row 7: Purl.
Row 8: (K2tog, k1) to end (10 sts).
Thread yarn through sts on needle, pull tight and secure by threading yarn a second time through sts.

Back of headdress

Beg at lower edge using the thumb method and F, cast on 22 sts.
Work 2 rows in garter st.
Beg with a k row, work 2 rows in st st knitting the first 2 and last 2 sts on the p row.
Row 5: K6, k2tog, k6, k2tog, k6 (20 sts).
Cont to make edging by knitting the first 2 and last 2 sts on every p row throughout and beg with a p row, work 3 rows in st st.
Row 9: K5, k2tog, k6, k2tog, k5 (18 sts).
Row 10: Purl.
Row 11: K4, k2tog, k6, k2tog, k4 (16 sts).
Cast off in patt.

Making up

Make up Body and Head, Base and Arms as for Noah.

Features

Work eyes and nose as for Noah and work mouth in red, taking a V-shaped stitch over two stitches on second and third row below nose at centre front (see p. 122 for beginning and fastening off embroidery invisibly). Shade cheeks with a red pencil.

Headdress

Join row ends of top of headdress and place on head; sew cast-on stitches to head all the way round. Sew cast-off stitches of back of headdress to lower edge of top of headdress from each side around back of head.

Belt

Make belt in F as for Noah.

ARK & RAINBOW

Information you'll need

Finished size
Ark measures 15in long and 13in high
(38 x 33cm)
Ramp measures 5½in (14cm) high
Rainbow measures 9½in (24cm) high

Materials for Ark and Ramp
Any DK (US: light worsted) yarn
(NB: amounts are approximate)
140g mid-brown (A)
40g dark brown (B)
80g fawn (C)
1 pair of 3.25mm (UK10:US3) needles
Knitters' blunt-ended pins and a needle
for sewing up
Acrylic toy stuffing

Materials for Rainbow
Any DK (US: light worsted) yarn
(NB: amounts are approximate)
20g red (A)
20g orange (B)
20g yellow (C)
20g green (D)
15g blue (E)
15g indigo (F)
15g violet (G)
1 pair of long 3.25mm (UK10:US3) needles
A needle for sewing up
Thick cardboard such as mounting board
approx. 20 x 12in (50 x 30cm) in size

Tension
26 sts x 34 rows to 4in (10cm) square over
st st using 3.25mm needles and DK yarn
before stuffing.

How to make Ark

Note: If casting on or off is narrower than the knitting, cast on or off more loosely or use a bigger needle.

Sides (make 2)

Beg at lower edge using the thumb method and A, cast on 90 sts for WS facing for first row.
Beg with a p row, work 7 rows in st st.
*Join on B and work 2 rows in garter st.
Cont in A and work 8 rows in st st.
Rejoining B, rep from * 3 times more.
Cont in B and work 20 rows in garter st.
Cast off.

Base

Beg at one end using the thumb method and A, cast on 16 sts.
Row 1 (WS): Purl.
Row 2: (K1, m1) twice, k to last 2 sts, (m1, k1) twice (20 sts).
Row 3: Purl.
Row 4: K1, m1, k to last st, m1, k1 (22 sts).
Rep last 2 rows 5 times more (32 sts).
Beg with a p row, work 3 rows in st st.
Row 18: K1, m1, k to last st, m1, k1 (34 sts).
Rep last 4 rows once (36 sts).
Beg with a p row, work 59 rows in st st.
Next row: K2tog, k to last 2 sts, k2tog tbl (34 sts).
Beg with a p row, work 3 rows in st st.
Rep last 4 rows once (32 sts).
Next row: K2tog, k to last 2 sts, k2tog tbl (30 sts).
Next row: Purl.
Rep last 2 rows 5 times more (20 sts).
Next row: (K2tog) twice, k to last 4 sts, k2tog, k2tog tbl (16 sts).
Purl 1 row.
Cast off.

Deck

Beg at one end using the thumb method and C, cast on 18 sts.
Row 1 (WS): Purl.
Row 2: (K1, m1) twice, k to last 2 sts, (m1, k1) twice (22 sts).
Rep first 2 rows 3 times more (34 sts).
Row 9: Purl.
Row 10: K1, m1, k to last st, m1, k1 (36 sts).
Rep last 2 rows twice (40 sts).
Beg with a p row, work 3 rows in st st.
Row 18: K1, m1, k to last st, m1, k1 (42 sts).
Beg with a p row, work 5 rows in st st.
Row 24: K1, m1, k to last st, m1, k1 (44 sts).
Beg with a p row, work 7 rows in st st.
Row 32: K1, m1, k to last st, m1, k1 (46 sts).
Beg with a p row, work 55 rows in st st.
Next row: K2tog, k to last 2 sts, k2tog tbl (44 sts).
Beg with a p row, work 7 rows in st st.
Next row: K2tog, k to last 2 sts, k2tog tbl (42 sts).
Beg with a p row, work 5 rows in st st.
Next row: K2tog, k to last 2 sts, k2tog tbl (40 sts).
Beg with a p row, work 3 rows in st st.
Next row: K2tog, k to last 2 sts, k2tog tbl (38 sts).
Next row: Purl.
Rep last 2 rows twice (34 sts).
Next row: (K2tog) twice, k to last 4 sts, k2tog, k2tog tbl (30 sts).
Next row: Purl.
Rep last 2 rows 3 times more (18 sts).
Cast off.

Cabin Back

Using the thumb method and C, cast on 40 sts for WS facing for first row.
Beg with a p row, work 35 rows in st st.
Cast off.

Cabin Ends (make 2)

Using the thumb method and C, cast on 21 sts.
Beg with a p row, work 37 rows in st st.
Row 38 (RS): K2tog, k to last 2 sts, k2tog tbl (19 sts).
Beg with a p row, work 3 rows in st st.
Rep last 4 rows 7 times more, then rep dec row once (3 sts).
Purl 1 row.
Next row: K3tog tbl (1 st).
Fasten off.

Cabin Front

For intarsia, wind a small ball of C, 100in (250cm) in length and divide rem C into 2 separate balls.
Using the thumb method and C (first ball), cast on 40 sts.
Work in intarsia and join on and break off colours as required, twisting yarn when changing colour to avoid a hole.
Row 1 (WS): Using C, p24, using A, p12, using C (second ball), p4.
Row 2: Using C, k4, using A, k12, using C, k24.
Row 3: Using C, p24, using A, p12, using C, p4.
Rep rows 2 and 3, 6 times more.
Row 16: Using C, k4, using A, k12, using C, k6, using B, k12, using C (small ball), k6.
Row 17: Using C, p6, using B, p12, using C, p6, using A, p12, using C, p4.
Rep rows 16 and 17, 6 times more.
Cont with 1 ball of C only and work 6 rows in st st.
Cast off.

Window Frame (make 4 pieces)

Using the thumb method and A, cast on 13 sts for RS facing for first row.

Row 1: Knit.

Cast off k-wise.

Door Handle

Using the thumb method and B, cast on 9 sts.

Thread yarn through sts on needle, pull tight and secure by threading yarn a second time through sts.

Cabin Roof (make 2 pieces)

Using the thumb method and B, cast on 40 sts for RS facing for first row and work in garter st.

Work 45 rows in garter st.

Cast off in garter st.

Making up

Ark Sides and Base

Place two pieces of ark sides together, matching all edges. Join row ends by sewing back and forth one stitch in from edge. Fold rim of ark over to inside and sew cast-off stitches in place. Pin base to lower edge of ark with seams of ark sides at the midpoint of cast-on and cast-off stitches of base. Sew round outside edge of base. Place the ark on a flat surface and stuff.

Deck

Sew deck to inside edge of ark at inside base of garter-stitch rim, all the way round.

Window Frame and Door Handle

Weave in loose ends around intarsia. Sew window frames around window using backstitch down centre of window-frame pieces. Sew door handle to door as shown in the picture on page 109.

Assemble Cabin and Cabin Roof

Join row ends of cabin sides and ends. Sew cast-off stitches of pieces of roof together, then pin and sew roof to cabin using backstitch on the right side. Stuff the cabin, place it on the deck and pin and sew the lower edge of the cabin to the deck all the way round.

How to make Ramp

Side Pieces (make 2)

Using the thumb method and A, cast on 52 sts.

Row 1 (WS): Purl.

Row 2: K2tog, k to last 2 sts, k2tog tbl (50 sts).

Row 3: P2tog tbl, p to last 2 sts, p2tog (48 sts).

Row 4: K2tog, k to last 2 sts, k2tog tbl (46 sts).

Rep rows 1 to 4, 7 times more (4 sts).

Purl 1 row.

Next row: K1, k2tog, k1 (3 sts).

Next row: P3tog tbl (1 st).

Fasten off.

Gusset Pieces (make 2)

Using the thumb method and A, cast on 20 sts for WS facing for first row.

Beg with a p row, work 45 rows in st st.

Cast off.

Ramp

Using the thumb method and A, cast on 20 sts for WS facing for first row.

Beg with a p row, work 3 rows in st st.

*Work 2 rows in garter st.

Work 4 rows in st st.

Rep from * 11 times more.

Cast off.

Making up

Assemble Ramp

Oversewing on right side, sew gusset pieces to short sides of side pieces and stuff. Sew ramp to open edge all the way round.

How to make Rainbow

Rainbow (make 2 pieces)

Using the thumb method and A, cast on 180 sts.

Row 1 (WS): Purl.

Row 2: (K18, k2tog) 4 times, k20 (k2tog, k18) 4 times (172 sts).

Row 3: Purl.

Change to B and work 2 rows in st st.

Row 6: (K17, k2tog) 4 times, k20, (k2tog, k17) 4 times (164 sts).

Row 7: Purl.

Change to C and work 2 rows in st st.

Row 10: (K16, k2tog) 4 times, k20, (K2tog, k16) 4 times (156 sts).

Row 11: Purl.

Change to D and work 2 rows in st st.

Row 14: (K15, k2tog) 4 times, k20, (k2tog, k15) 4 times (148 sts).

Row 15: Purl.

Change to E and work 2 rows in st st.

Row 18: (K14, k2tog) 4 times, k20, (k2tog, k14) 4 times (140 sts).

Row 19: Purl.

Change to F and work 2 rows in st st.

Row 22: (K13, k2tog) 4 times, k20, (k2tog, k13) 4 times (132 sts).

Row 23: Purl.

Change to G and work 2 rows in st st.

Row 26: (K12, k2tog) 4 times, k20, (k2tog, k12) 4 times (124 sts).

Row 27: Purl.

Cast off.

Making up

Rainbow

Place wrong sides of rainbow together, matching all edges. Join upper edge all the way round by oversewing on the right side. Place rainbow flat on a piece of cardboard and draw around the rainbow. Remove rainbow and make a bold, evenly curved line ¼in (6mm) inside drawn shape. Cut out on this bold line. Place cardboard piece inside the rainbow and finish joining row ends and lower edge of rainbow.

Techniques

Getting started

Buying yarn

All the patterns in this book are worked in double knitting yarn (DK yarn; known as light worsted in the US). There are many DK yarns on the market, from natural fibres to acrylic blends. Acrylic yarn is a good choice, as it washes without shrinking, although you should always follow the care instructions on the ball band. Be cautious about using a brushed or mohair-type yarn if the toy is intended for a baby or a very young child, as the fluffy fibres could be swallowed.

Tension

Tension is not critical when knitting toys if the correct yarn and needles are used. All the toys in this book are knitted on 3.25mm (UK10:US3) knitting needles. This should turn out at approximately 26 stitches and 34 rows over 4in (10cm) square. If you are using more than one colour in the design (for the giraffes or tigers, for example), it is advisable to use the same type of yarn for all the colours; some yarns are bulkier or finer, so your overall knitted fabric could turn out uneven.

Knitting techniques

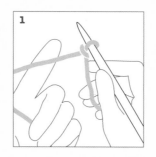
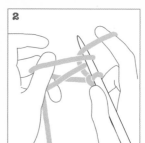

Slip knot

1 Leave a long length of yarn: as a rough guide, allow ⅜in (1cm) for each stitch to be cast on, plus an extra length for sewing up. Wind the yarn from the ball round your left index finger from front to back and then to front again. Slide the loop from your finger and pull the new loop through from the centre. Place this loop from back to front on to the needle that is in your right hand.

2 Pull the tail of yarn down to tighten the knot slightly and pull the yarn from the ball to form a loose knot.

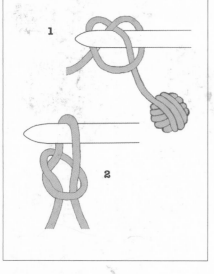

Casting on

Thumb method

1 Make a slip knot. Hold the needle in your right hand with your index finger on the slip knot loop to keep it in place.

2 Wrap the loose tail end round your left thumb, from front to back. Push the needle's point through the thumb loop from front to back. Wind the ball end of the yarn round the needle from left to right.

3 Pull the loop through the thumb loop, then remove your thumb. Gently pull the new loop tight using the tail yarn.

Repeat this process until the required number of stitches are on the needle.

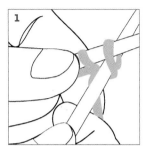
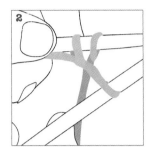

Cable method

When casting on part-way through knitting, such as for the tail of the cockerel or the gussets of many of the animals, the cable cast-on, a two-needle method, is used.

1 Work along the row to the point where the cast-on stitches are to be placed. Turn the work. Insert the right-hand needle from front to back between the first and second stitches on the left-hand needle and wrap the yarn around the tip of the right-hand needle from back to front.

2 Slide the right-hand needle through to the front to catch the new loop of yarn.

3 Place the new loop of yarn onto the left-hand needle, inserting the left-hand needle from front to back.

Repeat this process until you have the required number of cast-on stitches.

Turn the work once again and continue along row.

Knit stitch

1 Hold needle with stitches in left hand. Hold yarn at back of work and insert point of right-hand empty needle into the front loop of the first stitch. Wrap yarn around point of right-hand needle in a clockwise direction using your index finger. Bring yarn through to front of work.

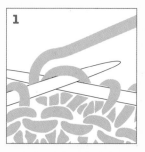

2 With yarn still wrapped around the point, bring the right-hand needle back towards you through the loop of the first stitch. Try to keep the free yarn fairly taut but not too slack or tight.

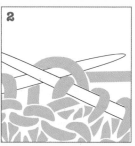

3 Finally, with the new stitch firmly on the right-hand needle, gently pull the old stitch to the right and off the tip of the left-hand needle. Repeat for all the knit stitches across the row.

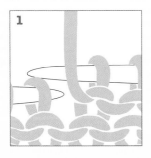
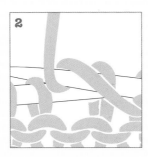
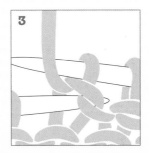

Purl stitch

1 Hold needles with stitches in left hand and hold yarn at front of work.

2 Insert point of right-hand empty needle into the front loop of the first stitch. Wrap yarn around point of right-hand needle in an anti-clockwise direction using index finger. Bring yarn back to front of work.

3 Now with yarn still wrapped around point of right-hand needle, bring it back through the stitch. Try to keep free yarn taut but not too slack or tight. Finally, with the new stitch firmly on the right-hand needle, gently pull the old stitch off the tip of the left-hand needle. Repeat for all the purl stitches along the row.

Types of stitch

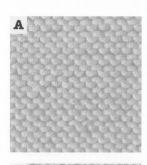

Garter stitch (A)
This is made by knitting every row.

Stocking stitch (B)
Probably the most commonly used stitch in knitting, this is created by knitting on the right side and purling on the wrong side.

Reverse stocking stitch (C)
This is made by purling on the right side and knitting on the wrong side.

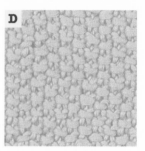

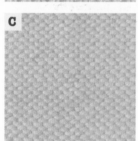

Moss stitch (D)
This stitch creates a bumpy-looking fabric made by alternating purl and knit stitches in a row. To create moss stitch, you need an odd number of stitches on the needle.

1 With the yarn at the back of the work, knit the first stitch in the normal way.

2 Purl the next stitch, but before you do so, bring the yarn through the two needles to the front of your work.

3 With the yarn now at the front, purl the stitch.

4 Next you need to knit a stitch, so take the yarn back between the needles and knit a stitch. Continue to k1, (p1, k1) to the end of the row. This row is repeated.

Increasing

Two methods are used in this book for increasing the number of stitches: inc and m1.

Inc – Knit twice into the next stitch. To do this on a knit row, simply knit into the next stitch but do not slip it off. Take the point of the right-hand needle around and knit again into the back of the stitch before removing the loop from the left-hand needle.

To do this on a purl row, purl first into the back of the stitch but do not slip it off. Purl again into the front of the stitch before removing the loop from the left-hand needle. You have now made two stitches out of one.

M1 – Make a stitch by picking up the horizontal loop between the needles and placing it onto the left-hand needle. Now knit into the back of it to twist it, or purl into the back of it on a purl row.

Decreasing

To decrease a stitch, simply knit two stitches together to make one stitch out of the two stitches, or if the instructions say k3tog, then knit three stitches together to make one out of the three stitches. To achieve a neat appearance to your finished work, this is done as follows.

At the beginning of a knit row and throughout the row, k2tog by knitting two stitches together through the front of the loops.

At the end of a knit row, if these are the very last two stitches in the row, then knit together through the back of the loops.

At the beginning of a purl row, if these are the very first stitches in the row, then purl together through the back of the loops. Purl two together along the rest of the row through the front of the loops.

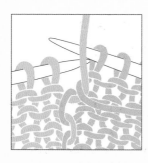

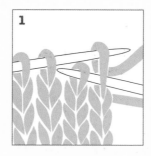

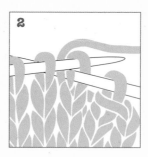

Intarsia

Blocks of colour are created by using the intarsia technique of twisting the yarns at the back of the work with each colour change (see diagram above). Once finished, weave in ends at the back of the work to prevent holes appearing between the beginnings and ends of the colour changes of the finished piece.

Casting off

1 Knit two stitches onto the right-hand needle, then slip the first stitch over the second and let it drop off the needle. One stitch remains.

2 Knit another stitch so you have two stitches on the right-hand needle again. Repeat the process until only one stitch is left on the left-hand needle. Break the yarn and thread it through the remaining stitch.

Fair Isle

Fair Isle knitting uses the stranding technique; this involves picking up and dropping yarns as they are needed, carrying the yarns along the wrong side of the row. These yarns must be carried loosely to avoid puckering.

1 Start knitting with the main colour (A), which is dropped when you need to change to the second colour (B). To pick up A again, bring A under B and knit again.

2 To pick up B again, drop A and bring B over A and knit again.

3 On the purl side, the same principle applies: start purling in A and carry B loosely across the back and under A and purl the next stitch.

4 To pick up A again, bring A over B and purl the next stitch.

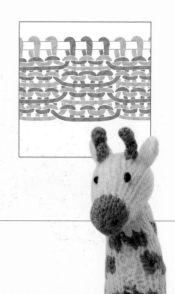

Sewing up

The animals and characters in this book are put together using simple sewing techniques.

Joining row ends
Pieces can be joined by oversewing on the wrong side and turning the piece the right side out. For smaller pieces or pieces that cannot be turned, oversew on the right side.

Joining striped row ends
Join row ends by sewing back and forth one stitch in from the edge on the wrong side.

Mattress stitch
Join row ends by taking small straight stitches back and forth on the right side of work (see diagram above left).

Backstitch
Bring the needle out at the start of the stitch line and take a small stitch, bringing the needle out a little further along. Insert the needle at the end of the first stitch and bring it out still further along. Continue in the same way to create a line of stitches.

Threading yarn through stitches

Sometimes the instructions will tell you to 'thread yarn through stitches on needle, pull tight and secure'. To do this, first break the yarn, leaving a long end, and thread a needle with this end. Pass the needle through all the stitches on the knitting needle, slipping each stitch off the knitting needle in turn. Draw the yarn through the stitches. To secure, pass the needle once again through all the stitches in a complete circle and pull tight.

Placing a marker

When placing a marker on the cast-on edge, thread a needle with yarn in a contrasting colour and count the number of stitches to where the marker is to be placed. Pass the needle between these stitches and tie a loose loop around the cast-on edge with a double knot and trim the ends.

To place a marker on a stitch, thread a needle with contrast yarn and pass this needle through the stitch on the knitting needle to be marked. Tie a loose loop with a double knot and trim the ends.

Finishing touches

Embroidery

To begin embroidery invisibly, tie a knot in the end of the yarn. Take a large stitch through the work, coming up to begin the embroidery. Allow the knot to disappear through the knitting and be caught in the stuffing. To fasten off invisibly, sew a few stitches back and forth through the work, inserting the needle where the yarn comes out.

Long stitches

Embroider nostrils and some mouths by sewing long stitches.

Backstitch

Bring the needle out at the beginning of the stitch line, make a straight stitch and bring the needle out slightly further along the stitch line. Insert the needle at the end of the first stitch and bring it out still further along the stitch line. Continue in the same way to create a line of joined stitches.

Making eyes

1 Make a loose single slip knot and then wind the yarn around three, four or five times as pattern states. (The diagram below shows the yarn being wound three times.) Pull the knot tight.

2 You now have an oval-shaped eye. Make two and check that the knots are the same size. Tie the eyes to the head in the position as stated in the instructions. Run the ends into the head.

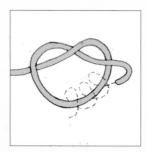

Making tassels

1 Take a piece of stiff card with a width that is the same as the length of the intended finished tassel plus 2in (5cm), and wrap the yarn around it several times. Secure this bundle with a separate length of yarn threaded through at one end leaving long ends, then cut the bundle at the opposite edge.

2 Keeping the bundle folded in half, wind a separate length of yarn a few times round the whole bundle, including the long ends of the tie, approximately ¾in (2cm) below the fold, to form the head of the tassel. Tie the two ends of this length of yarn together tightly. Trim all the ends of yarn at the base of the tassel to give a tidy finish. If you want to make a bushier tassel, unroll and separate the strands of yarn.

Making a twisted cord

A twisted cord is used for the pigs' tails and the belts for Noah and Mrs Noah.

1 Cut even strands of yarn to the number and length stated in the pattern and knot each end. Anchor one end – you could tie it to a door handle or a chair, or ask a friend to hold it.

2 Take the other end and twist until tightly wound.

3 Hold the centre of the cord, and place the two ends together. Release the centre, so the two halves twist together. Smooth it out and knot the ends together.

Stuffing & aftercare

Spend a little time stuffing your knitted figure evenly. Acrylic toy stuffing is ideal; use plenty, but not so much that it stretches the knitted fabric so the stuffing can be seen through the stitches. Fill out any base, keeping it flat so the figure will be able to stand upright. Tweezers are useful for stuffing small parts.

Washable filling is recommended for all the stuffed figures so that you can hand-wash them with a non-biological detergent. Do not spin or tumble dry, but gently squeeze the excess water out, arrange the figure into its original shape, and leave it to dry.

Abbreviations

alt	alternate
beg	beginning
dec	decrease/decreasing
DK	double knitting
foll	following
garter st	garter stitch: knit every row
inc	increase/increasing
k	knit
k2tog	knit two stitches together: if these are the very last in the row, then work together through back of loops
k3tog	knit three stitches together
k-wise	knit ways
LH	left hand
m1	make one stitch: pick up horizontal loop between the needles and work into the back of it
moss st	moss stitch: knit 1 stitch, (purl next stitch, knit next stitch) to end
patt	pattern
p	purl
p2tog	purl two stitches together: if these stitches are the very first in the row, then work together through back of loops
p3tog	purl three stitches together
p-wise	purl ways
rem	remaining
rep	repeat(ed)
rev st st	reverse stocking stitch: purl on the right side, knit on the wrong side
RH	right hand
RS	right side
s1k	slip one stitch knit ways
s1p	slip one stitch purl ways
st(s)	stitch(es)
st st	stocking-stitch: knit on the right side, purl on the wrong side
tbl	through back of loop(s)
tog	together
WS	wrong side
yf	yarn forward
yb	yarn back
( )	repeat instructions between brackets as many times as instructed
*	repeat from * as instructed

Conversions

Knitting needles

UK:	US:
10	3

Metric = 3.25mm

Yarn weight

UK:	US:
Double knitting	Light worsted

Terms

UK:	US:
Cast off	Bind off
Moss stitch	Seed stitch
Stocking stitch	Stockinette stitch
Tension	Gauge
Yarn forward	Yarn over

Suppliers

Sirdar Bonus DK
www.sirdar.co.uk
+44 (0)1924 371 501

About the author

Sarah Keen was born in Wales in the UK and has lived there all her life. She discovered the love of knitting at a very early age: her mother taught her when she was just four years old, and by the age of nine she was making jackets and jumpers.

Sarah has a diploma in Art and Design and now works as a freelance designer, knitting being her special interest. She is experienced in designing knitted toys, having made many for her nephews and nieces. She also enjoys writing patterns for charity and publishes them at home. Sarah is passionate about knitting and finds pattern writing and designing exciting and fascinating – and very addictive!

Acknowledgements

The author would like to thank:
Cheryl, Alison, Mary and Bethan and all supporting family and friends who have enquired and enthused about this book at all stages of its coming together.

Special thanks to Cynthia of Clare Wools (www.clarewools.co.uk) and thanks to all the team at GMC.

Index

To place an order, or to request a catalogue, contact:
GMC Publications Ltd
Castle Place, 166 High Street, Lewes, East Sussex BN7 1XU
United Kingdom
Tel: +44 (0)1273 488005
Website: www.gmcbooks.com